LIVING WITH SEVERE OCD

MARIE GIUS

BOOK PUBLISHERS NETWORK

Book Publishers Network
P.O. Box 2256
Bothell • WA • 98041
Ph • 425-483-3040

10 9 8 7 6 5 4 3 2

Printed in the United States of America

LCCN 2006927584
ISBN 1-887542-41-8

Editor/Proofreader: Julie Scandora
Cover Design: Laura Zugzda
Interior Layout: Stephanie Martindale

DEDICATION

I dedicate this book to all people with mental illness, especially those with obsessive compulsive disorder, or OCD. I offer my sincere thanks to all the professional mental health personnel who have assisted me, especially the following: Dr. Sony Taylor, Dr. Fred Montgomery, Dr. T. Jeffrey Stevens, Dr. Robert Permut, Dr. Donna Shaw, and Dr. James Salmon. Thank you, Dr. David Jaecks, internist, and Reverend Richard Sedlacek for your help and patience with me.

I am especially grateful to Dr. Dean Thompson, internist, who was my primary doctor from December 2001 to May 2005. As I have grown older, my OCD has become worse. Dr. Thompson made a special effort to help me feel that I stayed clean during my visits by not insisting I sit or lie on the examination table unless it was absolutely necessary. For example, when he listened to my cough for bronchitis, I was allowed to remain standing. He has made it possible for me not to have to take an extra shower every time I return from an appointment. A graduate of George Washington School of Medicine in Washington, D.C., he states, "I am motivated to help patients optimize their health and wellness."

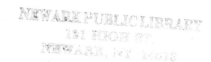

I also thank my close friends who have helped me cope with OCD over the years. Thanks to Barb, Gail, Lorraine, Lynnette, Nikki, Joanne, Sherry, and Linda, and to Della who has known about my illness for only a few weeks.

Most of all, I dedicate this book to my husband, Doug Spaulding, who is very understanding and loves me even if I act crazy.

I have purposely changed the names of some of the individuals mentioned to protect them. If there are any errors in the incidents I wrote about, I take full responsibility.

PROLOGUE

Mom never acknowledged that she had OCD. Every day she got dressed and stayed up all day even when she became very weak. Having OCD, Mom refused to lie down during the day because she didn't want to contaminate her bed with her dirty body. According to her inflexible routine, she would have had to change clothes before getting into her bed. Only near the end of her life did she allow herself to lie on top of her bed fully clothed. Mom had taught us – my older brother, Al, my identical twin, Leslie, and me – never to be on our beds unless we were in our pajamas, and she felt compelled to practice the same strange behavior. But toward the end, her need to get proper rest became too great; she finally knew she had to lie down without constantly changing from street clothes to bedclothes.

Mom died on December 25, 2005, from pancreatic cancer. She was diagnosed on August 9. On November 4, she was admitted to the hospital and then to the nursing home four days later. Since Mom was trained to be a registered nurse by nuns in the 1940's, she still felt until her dying day that she should never question a doctor. I know they are not gods, but Mom became upset with me for questioning their decisions, such as inquiring if her morphine should be increased. She would not tell the doctor the extent of her pain; however, she would tell Al, Leslie, and me. Even though she had been refusing more morphine, the doctor was able to convince Mom she needed more pain medication.

After Mom died, Leslie and I told some of her friends the hell we had been through growing up. I found out from Al that Mom never wanted him to play when he was a boy because she insisted his clothes stay clean. Imagine a young boy being told not to play because of cleanliness. One of Mom's best friends told me she remembers the first time Mom came to her house and would not put her purse on the floor. Many of Mom's friends knew there was something odd about the way we were raised, but they had no idea of the extreme behavior and rules we were forced to follow. The fact that all three of us did not want children bothered them the most, and some of her friends cried when they learned that.

Leslie told Ann, one of Mom's best friends, about an incident in sixth grade. "I can remember needing to go to the bathroom during class time. Fortunately, the bathroom was empty, but as I stood by the sink everything started moving, including the sinks, toilets, and mirrors. I was seeing germs everywhere, and I screamed and screamed and screamed. I rushed out of the bathroom and waited until I was home. Years later I realized that someone had heard me. God had heard me screaming."

My life at home was filled with what I later realized were bizarre events and instructions and rules. One was that we were not allowed to take showers everyday because Mom was worried about the septic tank overflowing. At least that is what she told us, but now I believe she just didn't think we needed to bathe every day. Having us shower only infrequently confused us because it conflicted with her obsession for cleanliness. OCD is indeed a mental illness. We took daily showers in physical education classes from seventh through tenth grade, but when we entered our junior year of high school, we wanted to continue taking daily showers. I felt awful when I wasn't allowed to shower. Later in Mom's life she would shower every day and let us do the same if we came home for a weekend. Mom was a child in the 1920's when people usually took one bath a week and believed bathing too often dried out the skin.

One day when I was visiting Mom in the nursing home, I told the social activities director that I had heard someone brought a dog to work. I told her I had OCD; she was very understanding as she knew people who also have the disorder. I asked if the dog could be kept in the office while I was there so it would not wander into the room.

Mom was embarrassed after she left and said, "Why did you have to tell her about your OCD?"

"I don't feel comfortable being here if a dog is running around. I'm not afraid to tell medical people about my mental illness because if anyone is going to understand me, they are; the staff should be the first to be cooperative."

"Well, you embarrassed me, Marie, by telling her about your problem."

"I'm sorry, Mom, but it's the only way I'll visit you."

My forthrightness made Mom uncomfortable. And my inability to attend to her irked her. Leslie was able to hold Mom's hand and help her straighten her blankets, but I couldn't. I felt everything in the nursing home was contaminated, and I would not touch anything.

Still, Mom asked the obvious. "Why can't you help me, Marie?"

"I'll get a nurse or aide for you, Mom, but you know I consider this place unsanitary."

"But can't you change? It's embarrassing when you get someone every time and won't help me yourself."

"I'm sorry, Mom, but I can't suddenly change 52 years of learned behavior."

As Mom's morphine was increased, she no longer scolded me for not helping her. I cried as I felt I was sinning in not helping my mom even though I know I was innocent because of my mental illness. I kissed her twice while she was in the nursing home, but I was careful not to touch anything but her face. I envied Leslie being able to help her. At least I was able to visit her because even being in a nursing home gives me panic attacks.

When a friend named Eva came to visit, I was sitting on a chair by Mom's bed. There wasn't another chair in the room, so she was going to sit on the closed lid of the bedside commode. I would never have done that, and I couldn't imagine anyone else doing it; it was just so terribly filthy.

"Please, Eva," I told her, "don't sit on the commode. It's not clean. I'll get another chair from the staff!"

An aide was walking by in the hallway, and I asked her for an additional chair. Eva was surprised that I was so upset, so I explained to her I have OCD.

She looked at me and said, "I know."

I was shocked she knew about my illness, but again, I think many people found out after I tried to commit suicide in June 2000. No one mentioned my suicide attempt to me, but apparently everyone knew about it. I had told my close friends, but I didn't tell anyone from my small hometown. I really love the anonymity of a huge population because unlike a small town, hardly anyone knows or cares about a person's personal life.

Shortly before Mom died, Leslie and I were talking to a dear friend and neighbor named Della. We told her about how we were raised, but we made her promise to keep it a secret until Mom died. I wanted to shout to everybody the hell we had suffered all of our lives, but, again, I wanted to wait until Mom died. I had told Leslie two years ago I was going to write a book, and her first reaction was, "May I help you write it?"

Even with that response, I know Leslie is going to be upset with me for writing about my experiences. Leslie lives in Quincy, a farming community in eastern Washington of about 5,000 where we grew up. She will be embarrassed when this book is published because everyone she knows will learn about us. She excessively worries about what others think. A lot of my parents' friends probably already knew something wasn't right with us three children, and this is just going to confirm those ideas.

Al lives in Idaho, and I don't believe this book will bother him. Al escaped most of Mom's cleanliness habits because he didn't have to clean the house as Leslie and I did.

I do and I don't care what others think. I have hidden my feelings for so long, and I now feel a commitment to tell my story. My close friends have known about my mental illness for years. I needed people I could talk to confidentially about my problems, and I have appreciated their support.

I had promised myself that I would not publish my story until Mom had died. It has been very difficult holding back because of the pain she put us three children through when we were growing up. For decades, I have wanted to share my story. I feel such relief now in releasing what I have had to hold inside.

But I also want my story of one suffering with OCD to give insight to the medical profession about what living with this disorder really means. I also hope this book will help everyone who does not have obsessive compulsive disorder to understand those of us suffering from this mental illness. If untreated, OCD develops into a lingering disease, becoming more severe with advancing age.

I will hold back no longer. The time for the telling has come. Today is January 11, 2006. Al is now 56, and Leslie and I are 52, and I am ready to publish.

Nothing said here can hurt Mom. May she rest in peace.

Introduction

I wish I could turn off my brain from the continual flow of thoughts which include the following:
... debilitating ... crippling ... germs ... dirt ... actions ... behaviors ... senseless ... distress ... time involved ... interferes ... compulsive activities ... anxiety ... born with OCD ... repetitive thoughts ... obsession ... clinical ... cleanliness ... grotesque .. .intrusive ... anxiety-induced thoughts ... rage ... dark side ... homicidal ... panic ... washing hands repeatedly ... God knew before born ... internalize ... actress ... disguise ... side effect inhibits sexual feeling ... denial ... silence ... unpleasant ... worry ... vicious ... silently screaming ... swearing ... dying ... screaming ... loudly ... excessive ... ritualized ... wash over and over ... faint ... weak ... dying ... heart attack ... fighting ... OCD ... not relaxed ... run ... scream ... hide ... weird ... crazy ... not normal ... don't look at me ... nightmares ... hate myself ... stop ... high dosage of medications ... overwhelmed ... suicide ... escape ... genetic ... environmental ... blame mom ... responsible for own actions ... not my fault ... sterilization ... hospitals ... don't touch ... wash hands ... counting washings ... habits ... quality of life ... don't blame Mom ... madness ... over and over again.. parent ... love ...

hate ... exposure ... prevention therapy ... behavior modification ... SSRI ... serotonin ... disease of doubt ... irrational ... impulses ... recurring ... chemicals in brain ... depression ... antidepressants ... floor dirty ... emotionally ... physically ... fears ... germ phobias ... chronic ... disease ... coping ... treatment ... strep throat ... Obsessive Compulsive Disorder.

*Great Spirit, grant that I may not criticize my
neighbor until I have walked a mile in his moccasins.*

~Anonymous

CHAPTER ONE

I have obsessive compulsive disorder or OCD. In the Middle Ages people with OCD were thought to be possessed by the devil; in Victorian times it was considered a form of madness. In modern times more people have become aware of OCD because it is explained in health classes, and the media have increased public awareness through the movie *As Good As It Gets* and the television series *Monk*.

An obsession is an idea, impulse, or thought that haunts a person. Because the idea never goes away, it is distressing and feels unnatural. A compulsion is a need to act in a rigid way. OCD used to be referred to as the "disease of doubt." My particular obsession is with cleanliness. My behavior is compulsive and irrational because I don't have any control over how I react to situations that bother me. At least I don't feel as if I am in control of my actions. It is an anxiety disorder because what I do is not normal behavior. Normal? Every psychologist and psychiatrist I have consulted says there is no model of what is considered normal. I disagree as I don't think I am normal. Is it normal to avoid persons, places, situations, animals, life in general?

I grew up in what, on the outside, seemed a normal family. I had two parents who were married for 44 years until my dad died of cancer in 1991. I have one brother named Albert (Al), who is almost four years older than I am, and I have an identical twin sister named Leslie. My name is Marie. My dad's name was Leslie (Les), and my Mom's name was Margaret. Our last name is Gius, pronounced GUY-us.

I can remember as a child I never watched where I was going and would bump into people because I was making sure I didn't step on any cracks in the sidewalk. This behavior can be an early sign of OCD.

Controlling obsessions and compulsions can be helped by cognitive behavior therapy, which changes existing patterns of behavior by altering how a person responds to his or her environment. Behavior therapy for OCD helps a person learn how to cope with fears while ridding him or herself of doing endless and useless rituals. There is no cure for OCD, but medications help to control the condition by lessening the anxiety associated with it. Participating in behavioral therapy helps a person confront the symptoms and then work on alleviating the rituals. It is not easy to be involved in behavior therapy as it produces high levels of anxiety, but it can help by decreasing the uncontrollable urges and symptoms. I have been in therapy sporadically since I was a freshman in college.

Doctors don't know what causes OCD, but genetics is thought to be at least partly responsible. The condition is known to be connected to low levels of serotonin in the brain. Serotonin is a natural chemical in the brain related to emotion in the nerves. Cells need serotonin to relay messages to each other to perform everyday functions such as talking and eating. Scientists have discovered people with OCD and depression tend to have lower amounts of serotonin between nerve cells. Medication helps keep the amount of serotonin level.

There are also newer studies that suggest a high correlation between identical twins who are sick with strep throat as children being very susceptible to OCD. Leslie and I had sore throats which turned into strep throat constantly when we were young. Strep antibodies (cells the body develops to bombard specific diseases) attack a part of the brain that results in generating excessive germ or washing phobias. We both had our tonsils removed at the age of seven. Having a tonsillectomy helped me to stay well, but it didn't prevent my getting strep throat. I still get sore throats, which quickly become strep throat if I am not careful.

I will always appreciate the excellent care Mom gave us, not only when we were sick but also when we were well. Mom dedicated her whole life to helping her family. Her care created conflict within me. I loved her for her dedication, but I hated her at the same time for making me be paranoid about everything.

So how did I get OCD? Genetics and the environment are both considered to be factors. My mom is an extreme worrier, and all three of us children are also. My mom was a registered nurse who once said that she entered that profession because she loved the smell of Lysol in the hospital. In the 1940's, grooming items were sterilized in hospitals before everything became disposable. She grew up in a very clean environment as her father was a dairy farmer who had to deal with health inspectors, but her siblings did not become obsessed with cleanliness as my mother did. When I was a child, Leslie and I had to soak combs and brushes in Lysol with water every Saturday; we would let them soak for an hour and then scrub the brushes and combs until our hands were raw and red.

Ever since I was old enough to remember anything, Mom constantly bombarded us with commands, "The floor is dirty. Never sit on the ground. Wash your hands. Don't touch babies; you'll contaminate them. Don't pet stray animals, and wash your hands after you touch a pet."

Leslie and I remember when a friend of Mom's had a newborn infant. We were nine and had just come out of church. We were excited to see the baby and went running towards it. Mom got upset and quickly pulled us back; we weren't allowed to touch or even get close. Is it any wonder that we three children chose never to have children of our own? My mom would constantly repeat the same rules over and over again: don't touch babies; you'll get them sick. Leslie told me years later that this incident had been the deciding factor – she would never have children.

In first grade our friends went to Camp Fire Girls after school was over. We would walk with them to the corner and then go home by ourselves. We wanted to be a part of their group and wear the uniforms. Mom forbade us from joining because she didn't want us going camping. For her, nature could not be controlled and kept sanitary. If she were not around to ensure that we stayed clean during outdoor play, then we would just have to avoid such environments altogether. But at the time, we couldn't understand why we were denied joining in our friends' fun activities and were saddened with such lost opportunities.

Until I turned eleven, Mom let us play in a dirt fort, make mud pies, ride our bicycles, play outdoor games, and do everything else children do. This seems inconsistent with Mom's regulations about cleanliness, and often her behavior was beyond the understanding of a child. I think that as long as we were at home, Mom could make sure we were given baths every night. But Al was not so fortunate. He was not allowed to play even at home; in her mind boys were too rough and would damage their clothes.

When Leslie and I turned ten, Mom and Dad thought we were old enough to take a two week vacation without being disruptive or bored. The summer of 1963 our family went to Yellowstone National Park in Wyoming. Every summer thereafter, we would travel by car to different western states.

In 1964 we were visiting my dad's cousin in Los Angeles. Cyril, his wife, and two sons lived in a beautiful home overlooking a canyon. They had two beagles named Clyde and George. Leslie and I wanted to go swimming in their pool, but Mom would only let us remove our socks and dangle our feet in the water. We were enjoying ourselves all the same when George grabbed our socks and took off. We thought this was funny, but Mom quickly put a damper on the dog's antics.

"Leslie and Marie, get your socks back and put them on!" cried Mom.

We quickly followed her orders, but were confused and unhappy with such restrictions on innocent fun.

In the summer of 1966, we drove to Alaska on the Alcan Highway. One night we stayed in a motel that did not have bathrooms in the rooms. We had to go down the hall and use the bathroom shared by everyone.

"This is intolerable!" Mom declared.

"We can't do anything about it, Margaret; it's the only motel available. You'll just have to make the best of it," said Dad.

Al, Leslie, and I weren't upset, as we were traveling and knew everything wasn't going to be perfect. When one is a youngster, everything is an adventure.

The effect of having a mother so obsessed with cleanliness eventually became evident to us. Leslie and I noticed we were somehow different from the other girls during fifth grade. I can remember not wanting to be in the bathroom at school if anyone else was there. If I heard a toilet flush, I was positive I had been sprayed by toilet water. I would be washing my hands and run away from the sink when I knew someone was coming out of a stall. I freaked when someone would wash her hands in the sink next to me. I'd been told to wash for 15 seconds to clean my hands. Most of the girls just turned on the water, ran their fingertips through the water, shook their hands, and reached for a paper towel. Grotesque! The girl standing next to me at another sink still did not have clean hands. Then she'd get water on me as she shook her hands. I felt so contaminated. I had to wait until everyone else had left the bathroom so I could properly clean myself. I was always late to class and everyone would look at me as if I were weird.

My obsession had another outlet besides ritual cleaning: perfectionism. In fifth grade, students went to separate classes for reading and vocabulary. I was placed in the highest class, but I was always the last one to finish my vocabulary because I would write in my own words every definition in the dictionary. Most students wrote only a few words, but I had to do more; I was a perfectionist. But my excessiveness didn't pay off. When I entered sixth grade, I was dropped a level in reading because of the amount of time it took me to finish my work.

I don't know how Leslie and I were able to have a horse in sixth grade, go with dad to cattle auctions, and go for boat rides on our boat that was kept in the garage where there were mice. We went to one slumber party when we were teens and were allowed to have a slumber party at our house, but it had to be in the garage, as Mom didn't want any sleeping bags in the living room. We seldom had friends come to the house because they couldn't relax. I know how they felt, as I was afraid to sit on the furniture, and I lived there.

In junior high physical education classes, bars of soap were provided for showers. Mom wouldn't let Leslie and me use the same soap everyone else was using. We each had to take our own soap in plastic containers. The other girls would always look at us as if we were crazy and say, "What's wrong with using the same soap? Do you think we have cooties or something?" Little did they realize how close to the truth they were.

As teenagers, we begged Dad to let us go to CYO (Catholic Youth Organization) summer camp in Leavenworth, which is located in a beautiful area in eastern Washington surrounded by mountains and huge evergreen trees. Mom was against us going, but Dad ruled we could go. Leslie and I thoroughly enjoyed camp. Jenny and I were chosen by the members of our cabin to be counselors for the day. Leslie was chosen by the counselors to be honor camper of our cabin and the session, and she was awarded a trophy for honor camper of the year. I was very proud of her because 250 girls (everyone who had gone to summer camp) were eligible for that award.

Dad helped temper Mom's obsession with all that was dirty. Dad told Leslie that if he had realized how my mother's obsession with cleaning was going to destroy his children, he would never have married her. He knew she was a neat housekeeper, but he had no idea how his wife's rituals would affect us three children.

As time passed, Dad became more aware that the three of us kids avoided participating in many activities that our peers did because we had such unreasonable fears of becoming contaminated. I finally told my parents during my sophomore year of high school that I could no longer take the garbage out. I explained that they could punish me if they wanted, but I could not cope being near the trash cans anymore. Dad and Mom understood how much this mattered to me, and they stopped making Leslie and me do this job. I was relieved they agreed to my request, but they also saw the routine I went through just to feel clean again after taking out the garbage. They probably felt it was not worth the rituals involved to make me do the chore.

Dad knew my problem was because of his wife, but he didn't know what to do about it. He was sad when I acted strangely. He couldn't understand why I was not able to function normally. We never talked about my behavior as I think both of us were too embarrassed to discuss my habits.

But Dad did have a softening influence. Besides letting us go to camp, Dad also had us help him with his commercial garden. In the summer between ninth and tenth grade, Dad planted nursery apple trees next to our house. Leslie and I were responsible for weeding, irrigating, and cutting weak limbs. We would start working at six in the morning when it was still cool. By eleven we would quit until two when the sun was less intense. Neither one of us wanted to be in the house when we were covered with dirt, so we stayed in the shade taking naps on blankets. Nursery trees are planted less than one foot apart. It takes patience to tend young trees as it would be very easy to destroy one with a hoe while weeding. We would crawl from one tree to another because it hurt our backs to keep standing. We carried long irrigation pipes above the trees and set the water to reach ten rows at a time. After two years, the nursery apple trees were replanted in a 60-acre orchard. Leslie and I were proud of ourselves because we earned our own money to buy contacts. It also gave us a sense of being normal to be working in the dirt.

During our junior and senior years of high school in 1970 and 1971, Dad had us working in the office of his farm implement business that he had owned with his partner, Joe, since 1952. Leslie and I filed, typed, totaled sales receipts, did the mail, helped with billing, and answered the phone. We loved working at the company because we had known the farmers all of our lives, and we were happy to help Dad.

The Quincy Valley, located geographically in the center of Washington State, produces over two hundred thousand acres of food for the nation. Grand Coulee Dam, a part of FDR's plans to put people back to work in the 1930's, was completed in the 1940's. All of the dams on the Columbia River turned a million acres of desert into irrigated land. The water finally filled the canals in Quincy in 1951. Leslie and I enjoyed helping the farmers. We have the greatest respect for them because they are agronomists, economists, and the biggest gamblers on earth.

CHAPTER TWO

Living with OCD made my life especially difficult during my high school years. When I think how I avoided activities in high school because of the fear of contamination, I realize how much fun I had missed. I purposely avoided going to basketball games because the bleachers were dirty; everyone was stepping on the bleachers which made them unclean to sit on. I didn't go to the annual parade because I didn't want to be near horses. I remember sitting behind a chair in our living room when I was 15 because I felt unclean. We had gone to a rodeo and returned home late. Mom would not let me take a shower after 10 p.m. While everyone else was sleeping, I was freezing. I didn't want to contaminate my bed or any other furniture.

In ninth grade home economics, Mrs. Elliott gave us an assignment about our homes. We had to list each room of the house and write how we used each room. She questioned Leslie and me when all we wrote for the bedroom was getting dressed and sleeping.

"Don't you listen to music or read in your rooms?"

"No," we replied, "we're not allowed to sit or lie on the beds, only sleep in them. And Mom won't let us sit on the rug. We have to study in the office or at the kitchen table."

In our freshman year of high school, Leslie and I were allowed to wear nylons, but Mom never told us about shaving our legs. One day in gym class, Marlene and Kristi set us straight. Leslie and I were embarrassed for not knowing and shocked for not having been told by Mom. I think Mom was trying to keep us from growing up too fast. She shaved her legs, but I believe she thought we were too young.

Young or not, I could take care of myself, even as a freshman. Once when I was walking down the school hallway between classes, Lewis, a senior, yelled, "There goes one of Al's twin sisters!"

Lewis was standing in the doorway of a classroom, looking at me with a smirk on his face.

I stopped and glared at him. "I want you to know, Lewis, that my brother is doing well in college, and he will probably be more successful in life than you will ever be. If you don't have anything better to do than pick on a freshman, you really have a problem. You can just leave me alone and go to hell!"

Astonished, Lewis just nodded at me as if he was thinking *Al's little sister knows how to defend herself.* Every time he saw me after that, he would look at me with respect.

Still there was much information that Dad and Mom held back from us, some minor as with shaving and some much more important. For instance, they never told us about sex and dating. We had to learn that from someone else. When Al came home at Thanksgiving during his freshman year of college, Leslie and I were sitting with him in the living room. He mentioned something about sex and noticed the blank looks on our faces.

"Twins, don't you know about sex?"

He told us, and so much suddenly made sense. *No wonder*, I thought, *men and women were so interested in each other.* And I thought about Dr. Jones visiting our eighth grade. He had talked to our class, but what he had said hadn't made sense to me at the time. I remembered him saying that "if a boy tells you he loves you in eighth grade, all he wants to do is get in your pants."

We were in the gym sitting on folding chairs, listening to this doctor and trying to understand what he was saying. The teachers were embarrassed; they stood around the perimeter of the gym, looking uncomfortable. I wish Dad and Mom would have prepared us for the world by giving us some background. I felt stupid being a ninth grader and not knowing the facts of life. Leslie was as surprised as I was, and we were glad our brother had enlightened us.

Besides making sense of that eighth-grade lecture, Al's talk helped us understand men. That information came in handy later that year when I visited his fraternity with my mom and dad for Parents' Day. One of his fraternity brothers, Aaron, grabbed my hand and said, "Come on. I want to take you upstairs and show you where I study."

Everyone was eating in the kitchen, and I was scared to be alone with Aaron. He was 20, and I was only 15.

"I don't want to go upstairs. Let go of my hand!"

"Ah, it won't hurt you to see the rest of the fraternity."

"No!"

Aaron kept pulling on my hand and wrist. I jerked my hand out of his reach and yelled, "Leave me alone! Why don't you pick on a girl your own age?"

Later, Aaron told my brother, "Hey, Al, your little sister knows how to take care of herself."

I had taken biology my sophomore year of high school and couldn't stand dissecting worms and frogs because in my mind they were dirty. The smell bothered me, and the formaldehyde made my contacts water. It reminded me of eighth grade science class when Mr. Pitts would walk down the rows of tables with a container of dead frogs. "Here, pick one!" he would exclaim with glee in his eyes.

Most of the girls in the class would balk, screaming, "Yuk!"

Mr. Pitts would throw a dead frog dripping in formaldehyde at anyone who acted squeamish. Formaldehyde splashed on my clothes as the dead frog landed on the table. I was glad I was still wearing glasses to protect my eyes from the chemical. I decided I would never have anything to do with the medical field as hospitals and the people in them are not very clean. I knew I could never work on a human cadaver because I would be disgusted by the smell and sight of internal organs; assisting sick people also made me nervous.

The students in the high school zoology class dissected cats that were laid out on huge trays. Since they had oral tests on the different parts of the cat every day, the students would take the cats home on the trays to study. They left these dead animals on shelves above the lockers used by all students. Why didn't they leave them in the zoology lab and pick up the dead cats before they went home? Because the students who rode buses didn't have time to go back to the lab after school was over and still make their bus. I detested being by the dead, dissected cats. Eventually I quit using my locker because the dead cats were only 16 inches above my head. Thinking my locker was contaminated by the dead cats, I felt everything inside my locker was also dirty.

I still had my consumer math book in my locker, but I wouldn't go near my locker. I told the teacher I needed another book. He didn't have any extras so in class I shared with someone else. Some of the students in my math class had just been in zoology, and their presence bothered me. If someone who had been dissecting cats wanted to borrow a pencil, I didn't want it back. If someone from zoology class had already touched a note I was asked to pass, I didn't want to help pass it. I usually finished my assignment before class was over, but then I felt it was contaminated. After class, I would go to the bathroom and throw my completed work away. The bathroom had wastebaskets that were wide and open so I did not have to touch anything. I would crunch my assignment into a ball and pretended I was shooting baskets in the gym. Most of the time it went into the trash can. If it didn't, I'd just leave it on the floor.

There were five minutes passing time between classes, and I would be in the bathroom grinding out Borax soap from the soap dispenser trying to get my hands washed and cleaned. The bell was ringing for the start of the next class and not only was I late, but my hands were completely white. It looked as if I was wearing gloves. I could rub my hands and the soap would fall off as if I were brushing away snowflakes. I was embarrassed, and I would always be hiding my hands. Items that I had touched before I washed my hands were contaminated so I had to throw them out, too. Of course, touching them in tossing them away would contaminate my hands, and I'd have to wash once again.

During high school I sometimes walked over to the football field and smoked with some friends during lunch. I also would smoke at home outside, but my parents didn't know. Although smoking is a dirty habit, filling the body with noxious substances, I never felt unclean smoking. I purposely didn't inhale correctly because I didn't want to become addicted and smoke the rest of my life. I again smoked when I was living in Hawaii and going to nightclubs; most of the time I would just light a cigarette and let it burn in the ashtray. I thought at the time it made me look sophisticated.

When my OCD was affecting me, life was difficult. But in my teen years, my OCD was not constant and ever-present. Sometimes I was hardly aware of it, and my life even seemed normal. Although I never had the chance to date boys in high school, the idea appealed to me and my OCD didn't prevent me from considering touching – or being touched by – members of the opposite sex.

In the spring of our junior year, my friend Lori decided to run for secretary of the senior class. She asked me if I would be a part of a skit she was doing for her campaign. I'd have to be willing to perform in an assembly before the whole school. I readily agreed. She explained that she'd have three girls being interviewed for a secretarial job by a good-looking guy. None of them would be qualified. She'd come out last and be the most capable.

I knew a really cute senior named Joe, who was going with Tricia. Joe was an easy-going person who was very friendly. Leslie and I had met him because he was on the same school bus everyday. I asked if he'd be part of the skit for Lori, and Joe said he was willing to help out.

The election assembly started at 10:00 on a Thursday. Jane walked out to the middle of the gym floor and sat in a chair opposite Joe's desk. She purposely acted silly.

"Thanks for your time, Jane. I'll let you know my decision in a week."

Edith interviewed next. She tripped over the chair and started howling. Horrified, she ran away from Joe.

I was the third secretary, the big flirt. I wore a velvet skirt with a frilly blouse and high heels. I sauntered out to the middle of the gym floor, went around the desk, put my arms around Joe, and sat in his lap. Joe looked at the students and grinned.

Students started yelling, "Ah, Joe!" They also turned around and looked at Leslie with a question in their eyes. Leslie was so embarrassed she wanted to sink below the bleachers. The teachers looked shocked!

"Hi, my name is Marie, and I'm applying for the secretarial position."

Joe smiled wickedly at me and said, "How fast can you type and take shorthand?"

"Well, I type only about 30 words a minute, and I don't know shorthand. But I do know how to do other things."

"Ah, Joe!" screamed the audience.

"I'll let you know my decision next week."

I stood up, turned, and smiled at Joe, and sauntered off while the students kept howling.

Lori appeared as "Miss Prim and Proper."

"What are your secretarial skills?"

"I type 80 words a minute. I can take shorthand. And I keep the office running smoothly. I'm the perfect candidate for you."

I got a lot of attention from my part, but unfortunately, Lori lost the election.

My OCD hadn't kept me out of Joe's lap, but soon after I had panic attacks again. I thought everything in school was dirty, including people because they were around the dead cats. I would avoid everyone as if they had a contagious disease. My grades started to slip, and I was not doing well in class. It was driving me crazy. I would pretend I was sick, so I wouldn't have to go to school every day. I think Mom let me stay home because she was lonely during the day. Leslie also started missing a lot of classes. If I stayed home, it meant one more day of not having to face the world and being afraid of getting dirty.

I was on the honor roll and in honor society in junior high, but in high school I didn't study as much as I should have studied. Throwing away my assignments because they were contaminated didn't help my GPA either.

My coping abilities at home and school were becoming intolerable. I was now washing my arms past my elbows to feel clean. I might as well have been a doctor prepping for surgery the way I washed so obsessively. My problem was obvious to others, but they were at a loss for what to do to help. One day Mom yelled at me through the locked bathroom door to stop washing my hands.

"Open this door immediately!" she screamed.

I kept on washing my hands and ignored her.

She roared, "Open this door, or I'll kick it in!"

I still didn't open the door, and Mom kicked a big hole in the door. Kicking the door seemed to take most of the anger out of her. When I opened the door, she just yelled at me, but she didn't hit me. I knew I needed help, but I didn't know where or how to get it. My mom and dad didn't know what was wrong with me besides the obvious fact of my being obsessed with cleanliness. We lived in a small town with only one high school counselor who assisted seniors with college applications. No one really understood what was going on inside me. There was no one I could talk to who could help me.

CHAPTER THREE

One day in the spring of my senior year of high school, I exploded. I yelled at Mom when she rebuked me for my washing habits while I was helping her cook dinner.

"I can't stand it anymore! You made me the way I am! It's all your fault that I'm such a freak!"

My explosion lit Mom's fuse. She was not a violent person, but she, too, couldn't take it any more. She started hitting me, and I crouched in the corner of the kitchen, putting my hands above my head to ward off her blows.

This was the scene my dad walked into when he came home for dinner. He separated us and took me to the den. I was crying hysterically and screamed, "Dad, I don't know how much more of this I can take. I'm going crazy."

Dad didn't know what to do, but he made me promise to get help when I went to Western Washington University in Bellingham that fall in 1971. I told him I would go to the counseling office the first week I was on campus. I walked into the psychology department the third day. "I need to see a psychiatrist," I announced to the receptionist.

"We don't have any psychiatrists, but you can see a psychologist."

"What's the difference between a psychiatrist and a psychologist? I thought they're both doctors."

"They are. But a psychologist has a degree only in psychology, not in medicine. A psychiatrist is a medical doctor who specializes in psychiatry. Only a psychiatrist can prescribe medication. It requires many more years of schooling to become a psychiatrist."

"Will a psychologist be able to help me? I wash my hands constantly. I can't stop myself. I have rituals that I have to do so I feel I'm staying clean."

I had to wait a week for my first session with Dr. Sony Taylor, who was in her early 30's and had a pleasant personality.

She said, "Marie, I want you to feel relaxed and just tell me as much as you can about how you are feeling. Don't rush and don't feel intimidated by me or any of your surroundings."

"Okay. Mostly I feel I'm going crazy because I wash my hands all the time. I avoid everything that I think could contaminate me. I have a procedure that I follow when I wash, and I hate myself because I can't stop myself from washing my hands and avoiding everything. I need help to deal with this condition. I avoid going outside because there are dogs, other animals, mud puddles, almost anything you can think of relating to dirt and germs that bothers me."

"Do you know what your condition is called?" Dr. Taylor asked.

"No, I just know I need help."

"You have a medical condition known as obsessive compulsive disorder, better known by the acronym OCD. I can help you cope with this disorder if you are willing to listen and follow my instructions."

At last I had a name to describe my problem or, as I like to think of it, my craziness. Maybe I wasn't a hopeless case after all if psychology had a name for what I thought of as craziness. I have always had an insatiable thirst for knowledge, and I was determined to learn everything I could about this mental illness.

"OCD. I've never heard of it before now," I replied with a look of wonderment on my face.

"I want you to see me twice a week for the next few weeks. As you progress in your treatment, I may have you come in for a session only once a week. Now tell me what you do so I can understand where you are and what coping skills you need to help you with this disorder."

"I don't even know where to begin, so I guess I'll just start as far back as I know. My grandfather came from Switzerland and started a dairy with a complete processing plant for pasteurizing the milk near Puyallup, Washington. He got married and had four children. My mom is one of those four children; she was born in 1921. Grandpa had to be very careful about cleanliness as the health inspectors would shut a dairy down if there were any unsanitary conditions. He told his children that they couldn't litter on the farm; not even a gum wrapper was to be left on the ground. Somehow, Mom's brothers and sister didn't become obsessed with cleanliness, but my mom did."

I took a deep breath and thought how good it felt finally to be telling someone my story and what I was experiencing.

"My brother, my identical twin, and I were told to wash our hands all the time. Because our brother, Al, didn't have to do housework, he avoided most of the habits my mom taught us. Leslie and I can remember being told we shouldn't touch any animals, the floor is dirty, and almost everything is contaminated. We were 11 when we started noticing we were different because of these crazy rules. I've been very angry with my mom since my junior year of high school. And I'm still angry."

I explained to Dr. Taylor about not wanting to be in the bathroom at school when others were present, and why Leslie and I felt strange in gym class because we weren't allowed to use the bar soap used by everyone else.

"I avoided athletic events because I didn't want to sit on the dirty bleachers. I was avoiding going anywhere or doing anything beyond going to school. I eventually didn't want to go to school either as it caused too much stress."

My next session was in two days, and I couldn't wait for it to start. I was finally getting the chance to talk to someone who was empathic about my problem. I was 18, and I had never had the chance to talk about what I was experiencing except with Leslie and my dad. They couldn't help me because they didn't know what I was trying to cope with, although Leslie had most of the same phobias. I loved to be with my twin, but I also found out it was not helpful for us to be around each other for any length of time as we would reinforce each other with our rituals. I would tell Leslie how something would bother me that she had not thought of before, and then she would be bothered by it, too. This also happened to me as she would relate events that I'd never thought of as being a source of contamination, and then, thanks to her, I would also think they were dirty. For example, she made me realize babies were dirty because they are always on the floor and in diapers. I told her I thought people in wheelchairs were not as clean as they could be because they used their hands to turn the wheels of their chairs, and she started avoiding handicapped people. We made each other crazy. Leslie would get mad at me because she thought I was acting weird, and I would get upset with her for doing something that bothered me. It's not easy to avoid a person that is so close to you. And it's very hard to ignore strange behavior that one's identical twin is doing when other people are around.

"Quit staring at the ground!" Leslie once yelled at me. "People are looking at you like you're weird."

"I can't help it because I see something on the ground that looks awful," I replied. "Don't worry if people are staring. They're looking only at me, not you."

"It doesn't matter which one of us they're seeing, Marie. Don't you get it? If you're acting weird, people are going to think I'm weird too."

Leslie and I loved each other, but when we were fighting, nine times out of ten, it had something to do with our OCD even though we didn't know the medical term for our problem. That is why I couldn't wait to see Dr. Taylor again and why Leslie and I didn't want to go the same colleges after we graduated from high school. We both needed our own space, and we both needed to feel we could act normal.

However, being an identical twin also was fun. We switched places in seventh grade one day, and the teachers didn't know it until someone told them.

Mrs. Tanwort, my homeroom teacher, said to me in a hostile tone, "Leslie took a pop quiz for you, and she flunked it because it was on the weekly magazine that you got but she hasn't received yet."

I couldn't stand her and didn't care that Leslie had flunked a silly quiz.

"I don't care; it doesn't bother me," I flippantly responded.

Mrs. Tanwort stood with her mouth agape. I was being a brat, and we both knew it.

The next day, Jean, an eighth grader who was very responsible for her age, told me that I was being considered as a candidate for the honor society for next year. But Mrs. Tanwort, who was the sponsor for the group, had decided to eliminate me from the list.

"I really think you should apologize to her," suggested Jean.

"I know I was disrespectful, but I hated how she snapped at me. Leslie and I were just having fun fooling the teachers," I replied.

"Now, Marie, if you're concerned about your future, you need to do the right thing and apologize."

Jean convinced me, and I did apologize. Years later at the 2000 year reunion for the classes of 1970 and 1971, I thanked her for helping me behave.

When I saw Dr. Taylor again, I told her about more of my crazy rituals.

"Mom said never to sit on a public toilet so I have to put three layers of toilet paper on the seat before I can sit down. It has to be a clean toilet, or I won't use it at all. I know there are germs on the toilet, but as long as I can't see them and the toilet looks clean, I can use it. When I stand up after going to the bathroom, all of the toilet paper falls to the floor. I won't touch it as it's dirty and so is the floor. It's embarrassing to use the bathroom in the dorm because of all the paper left on the floor of the stall. I know other girls are picking up the paper as it is usually gone by the next time I go to the bathroom.

"I also panic if I have to be around garbage or a garbage truck. If I'm by a garbage truck, I want to put my clothes in the laundry, throw away anything I was carrying at the time, and take a shower. I want to toss out everything I think is contaminated. But I can't do this in college, or I won't have any textbooks or my notes or my assignments. I'd flunk. Somehow I'll have to convince myself that my books and notebooks aren't dirty. I used to throw away assignments in high school, and my grades got low. I wash my hands about 20 times a day, and I will stand at the sink washing over and over again until I feel faint."

"Marie, I want to start you on some relaxation techniques to help you cope with public bathrooms and garbage trucks. Sit back and close your eyes. Imagine you are in a place that's very peaceful for you such as the ocean or the mountains. Now breathe in and out very slowly, taking deep breaths. Put your hands on the arms of the chair, and spread your fingers out. Imagine all that stress is leaving you through the tips of your fingers. Relax, breathe, relax, breathe."

It felt good to close my eyes and not worry about anything. I practiced this routine several times. Dr. Taylor also started role-playing therapy with me.

"Imagine yourself in a stressful situation such as being in a public bathroom. Now in your mind, approach the toilet. Are you visualizing the toilet? Is it what you consider a clean toilet? Keep getting closer to the toilet. Now imagine sitting down on the seat without putting toilet paper on it first. Keep telling yourself that the toilet is clean, and it doesn't need any paper on it."

Every time I went into a public bathroom I would have a panic attack. It took me three months of these sessions before I could finally sit on a public toilet seat without covering it with paper first. It was a relief finally to quit putting layers of toilet paper on the seat. I no longer had to worry about paper being on the floor anymore. This really helped me in the dorm and other public bathrooms.

CHAPTER FOUR

During the next session, Dr. Taylor had me visualize walking on the sidewalk.

"You are just returning from class with your books and notebooks, and you see a garbage truck coming towards you. Now, Marie, I want you to sit comfortably, close your eyes, take a few deep breaths, and when you start feeling stressed, I want you to make your hands into fists."

"Do you want me to gradually tighten my fists?"

"No, if you feel very stressed, make tight fists immediately. However, if I mention something that is only slightly stressful, gradually clinch your hands to show me how you are coping with the situation."

I nodded that I understood. I closed my eyes, took some deep breaths, and tried to relax.

"A garbage truck is in the lane right next to the sidewalk. It's an older garbage truck with the back part of the truck open, showing all of the gunk."

I immediately tightened my fists and was shaking.

"Okay, Marie, that's fine. Now visualize that the truck is going in the opposite direction. It's not right next to you.

It's a sunny day, and you can't see the back of the truck unless you turn around."

My hands tightened into fists, and I was still shaking.

"The next situation takes place in the dorm in the bathroom. You're washing your hands, and a girl puts clothes in the sink next to you. She's splashing water, and it's beginning to drip onto the floor."

I clenched my hands without shaking.

"Let's go on to another situation. You are walking down the street, and a dog is coming towards you. It's a clean-looking dog, not covered with dirt or wet from being in the rain."

I clenched my hands, but I was not shaking or making fists.

"Now you are sitting in the waiting room, and someone comes in with a seeing-eye dog and sits two chairs away from you. This time continue tightening your hands, but also tell me what you would do."

"I would leave immediately or go as far away from the area of the waiting room where the dog was sitting. I might even get brave enough to ask the receptionist to put me in a separate room while I was waiting to be seen."

"You forgot to clench your fists. What degree of tightness would being by the dog cause?"

I clenched my fists so hard I was shaking.

"Now, in the next situation a person picks up something from the floor and gives it to you."

I was shaking so hard I almost fell off the chair.

"I would need to wash my hands, but I would not have to take a shower if the object from the floor only touched my hands and not the rest of me. I would be careful not to touch any other part of me until I could wash my hands. For instance, if my hand accidentally touched my knee, I would need to take a shower as I feel I could not get my knee clean enough without showering. If someone put something on my lap, I would feel the need to put my clothes in the laundry and take a shower. I would feel contaminated until I was clean again."

At the end of the session, Dr. Taylor asked me if I had any questions or concerns.

"I know I told you I relate everything, but I don't know if I explained it very well. When I say I relate everything, I mean that I see the connections from what people have done some time before I encounter them. It's not just what they're doing when I am with them. For instance, if a person touched a dog and then sat in a chair, I wouldn't want to sit in that chair. It's now dirty from the dog. This drives me crazy."

"Yes, Marie, I understand. This is called displacement. We'll be working on that, too. For now I want you to keep a record of the number of times you wash your hands and the revolutions you make washing. For instance, if you wash up to or past your elbows, write it down. Write down how many times you rinse and use soap, and how long it takes each time to wash your hands. I want you to time yourself and record the minutes. We'll make a master chart that we'll keep here in my office. I also want you to record the time of day or night that you wash."

"I suppose I could do that although it sounds like a lot of record keeping."

"Believe me, Marie, there is a reason for everything I have you do. Why do you think I would want you to record this information?"

"I think you want me to become more aware of my actions and what my compulsions force me to do."

"That is exactly the reason. Part of this process is to help you get to the point of extinction where you no longer perform these behaviors. Record keeping helps you realize the amount of time you spend on them."

When the next session begin, I gave Dr. Taylor a record of my hand washings, showing the amount of time, revolutions made, and the number of times I had to wash and rinse. Keeping track had been tedious and time consuming, but it made me more aware of the obsessive compulsions I forced myself to do. One girl in our dorm was even worse than I was. Thankfully, she lived on the second floor, not the first floor where I lived. Two people with compulsory hand washing using the same bathroom would have been too much to endure. Her condition was worse than mine because she would wash her face several times until her face was shiny, and she would put her shoes up on the counter and constantly clean them. I never wanted to touch my shoes if I could help it. Many people with OCD buy only slip-ons so they don't have to wash their hands one more time from touching shoes.

Dr. Taylor continued working with me on my unrealistic fear of garbage trucks. By the third month of college, I was able to walk down the sidewalk without running in the opposite direction if a garbage truck was approaching. I was able to do this provided I did not get too close to the truck and it was not raining. If it was raining, I felt the rain that fell on the garbage truck also fell on me and, of course, contaminated me.

I was glad I was seeing Dr. Taylor. Finally having someone I could talk to about my problem and who understood me made such a difference in how I felt. I was so relieved. And having a name for my obsession made me feel less weird; others experienced this, too; I was not alone. And I was improving. I could see that I wasn't so extreme in my behavior. Until I came to Dr. Taylor, I had been drowning; for me, she was my lifeline.

While I was in college, I became more interested in psychology. I learned that B.F. Skinner's work with positive and negative reinforcement was a technique that Dr. Taylor used with me. I wondered if it was a good idea that I was learning about what my treatment would involve. I remember hearing that a surgical patient was more relaxed if he didn't know all the risks and what could go wrong during surgery. I couldn't stop myself from learning all I could as I was fascinated by the process involved to help me get better.

Dr. Taylor continued to help me deal with many aspects of campus life.

"Do you have any problems with your roommate because of your OCD? Does she have any concerns about your being her roommate?"

"My first roommate wasn't happy being in college and quit before Thanksgiving break. I was devastated until my resident aide, Linda, told me that it wasn't my fault that she had left. But she also told me I had two weeks to get another roommate or pay more for housing.

"I thanked Linda for telling me it wasn't my fault that my roommate had gone home. I actually wasn't surprised that she left. From the very first day I met her, she seemed unhappy. College is enough of a transition without being upset and feeling like you don't belong here at this time in your life."

"What was bothering your first roommate?" Dr. Taylor inquired.

"I don't know. We never had a chance to become good friends.

"I took my time deciding who to ask to be my new roommate. A girl named Lorraine was in my speech class and also attended Catholic mass at the campus ministry house. We had talked to each other a few times. I asked Lorraine if she got along well with her roommate.

"She said not that well; they didn't have much in common, and she liked to smoke in the room, which bothered Lorraine's eyes. When I asked if Lorraine wanted to be my new roommate, she didn't hesitate; we became roommates the same day. We've become good friends, and I've told her about my OCD. She's very understanding. Her mom is a nurse like my mom so Lorraine understands about my mom's need for cleanliness."

"I'm glad," Dr. Taylor said, "that Lorraine and you get along so well. By the way, I've been wanting to talk to you about sex and how it relates to your OCD. Would it embarrass you to talk about sex?"

"No, it doesn't bother me."

Since I had never dated in high school, I decided to make up for lost time and date when I started college. I went to a lot of parties. Linda told me that you can't go back and live what you have missed, but I thought I'd try.

By winter quarter of my freshman year, Linda's words rang true, and I was tired of partying. I still went to parties but only on weekends. When I would drink beer, my OCD wouldn't bother me. I could act in a way I considered normal and have a good time. But it was really hard for me to deal with my OCD when I was sober again. I would take hours to feel clean after I came home from a party. If I felt too dirty to touch my clean bed, I would sleep on the rug as I didn't want my clothes to contaminate my bed. I wouldn't be able to sleep most of the night because I was cold and uncomfortable.

I was also getting tired of dating. It was becoming exhausting and had little point for me. Although I had dated, I never wanted to keep the relationship going for very long as I was afraid the guy would realize I was weird. If I was on a date and we were sitting on a couch and the guy crossed his leg so the bottom of his shoe was towards me, I would feel dirty. I was so nervous of accidentally touching his shoe. Many people, when they're sitting, cross their legs and hold on to their shoe. I wasn't going to let some guy touch me who had just touched the bottom of his shoe. I could hear my mom saying, "The floor is dirty. Wash your hands. Don't touch anything." It was just easier for me not to get involved with one person for any length of time. I didn't want anyone saying, "Marie is so weird."

Dr. Taylor's words brought me back to the present. "First of all, Marie, I want to know if you consider kissing a guy dirty."

"No, that does not bother me in the least although I have kissed only about five guys in my life."

"The reason I asked you was because of the physical contact. You know that the mouth can contain germs also. How about anything having to do with being close to a guy?"

"If you mean holding someone, that doesn't bother me. I've never done anything else because I only started dating when I came to college. I think I would probably consider sex dirty because you have your clothes off and you're right next to a man. I don't think it's dirty as far as being wrong although at this point in my life I'm not ready to have sex without marriage. I don't think I have to worry about getting married; who would want to marry someone with my problem?"

"Marie, if the right person comes along, he will be able to accept you the way you are."

I didn't respond to her, but I didn't believe her. The chance of someone accepting me was beyond my comprehension. I was a nervous wreck. I was always in a state of panic, and if someone came up to me without my knowing it, I would scream loudly because I was startled. I had panic attacks all the time. I would imagine being on a date at a fast-food place and the guy throwing away the leftovers in one of the inside garbage bins that say "thank you." The guy had touched the dirty garbage container and then would want to hold my hand? No way!

"How do you feel about your mother now that you have been in therapy?"

"I still hate her, and I still blame her. She's the reason I'm the way I am. It'll be a big step if I ever get to the point where I stop blaming her and I can love her again. If I had another mother, I would be perfectly normal."

"You don't consider yourself normal after the sessions we have been through?"

"Of course not; do you consider me normal?"

"Yes, you are normal. You have a problem that needs to be dealt with, but you are a normal human being. You are intelligent, pleasant to be around, and like many others, struggling with personal problems."

Beginning with Dr. Taylor, all the psychologists and psychiatrists I have seen have told me there is no such thing as normal. I still don't believe them as I do not consider myself normal, just weird.

"Well, now that's an interesting way of putting it. But I don't buy it. I'm so afraid of everything. I figure if a guy really knew me, he'd laugh at me. I mean, what kind of guy with any brains at all would want to be around someone like me? I know I have a very low self-image, but for a good reason. I don't feel I'm important enough to bother with when there are plenty of other girls out there who are cute, smart, and NORMAL. Maybe I'm wrong, but I can't get away from my thoughts."

"You ignore guys because you're afraid they'll discover your secret. How about girls? Do you also stay away from them?"

"I have a lot of friends that are both guys and girls, but I make sure I never become too close to anyone. There's too much risk of them finding out what I'm really like."

"Let's just say a close friend did find about your OCD. What do you think he or she would do?"

"He or she would probably not want to have anything to do with me anymore. I'm afraid the person would talk about me to others. I couldn't take it if I saw people whispering about me."

"You certainly don't give the human race much credit for being sympathetic or understanding of another's problem. What about a situation where someone drinks, gambles, or whatever. How do you feel about people with those problems?"

"I feel sorry for them. I try and look at the whole person and find out why a person is doing the destructive behavior. Something must have caused an individual to become an alcoholic, a gambler, or whatever."

"Oh, so you're saying that you can accept problems in others, but no one could possibly understand your situation or be your friend if he or she found out about your OCD."

"Yeah, that's what I am saying. Do you think I'm short-changing the human race with my attitude?"

"How do you feel about that question? Do you think you are being fair to others?"

I took a deep breath and replied, "I guess I'm not being fair, but I am not willing to take the chance of finding out. Do you know how difficult it was for me to force myself to come into the counseling office and start seeing someone? I came because I knew I couldn't handle this problem by myself anymore; you were my last hope. I feel lucky the receptionist assigned me to you."

"That didn't happen by chance, Marie. We as a staff decided who would be the best person for you to see, considering your age, sex, and condition."

"Well, I'm still glad it was you, Dr. Taylor, because you've been a tremendous help to me."

"Thank you, Marie. I enjoy working with you. Do you have anymore to say about my question of being fair to others?"

"I'm beginning to realize I haven't put much faith in human nature. I know the first step to solving any problem is recognizing a problem exists. I had to admit to myself I needed help with OCD just like an alcoholic has to admit he has a drinking problem. It's unbelievable to me you were able to get me not to automatically take a shower because a garbage truck is near. I also think it's a miracle I no longer put paper on a toilet seat before I sit down if the toilet seat looks clean. I know it isn't really clean, but if it looks clean, I can now use a public bathroom."

"Marie, you've progressed more than you think. To be able to talk about your OCD and be willing to go through steps to help yourself takes a lot of effort and courage."

"To tell you the truth, Dr. Taylor, I don't think I will ever be cured from my mental illness. I'll probably die having this disorder. I can cope with the rituals better now than before because I know what my disorder is and how it affects me. You probably think I'm being very cynical and I should think positively, not negatively."

"That's right. If you assume you will always be helpless and can't continue to improve, you probably will stall in your treatment. Let's take one step at a time and see how you progress. Don't worry about the future right now; take care of the present. Do you think you can continue to get well if you try?"

"I don't know, but I'll try. There isn't a moment when I'm awake that I'm not worried about getting contaminated by something. I only relax when I'm sleeping or I've been partying and drunk enough so I don't care. Sometimes I'm afraid I might become an alcoholic because when I drink, I can relax and have a non-caring attitude. I don't care if I feel dirty. But I guess that isn't true either because no matter how much I have drunk, I still don't want to sit or lie down on my clean bed if I feel unclean. I don't drink unless I go to a party, and since I am a freshman in college, I go to a lot of parties. I don't want you to think I drink all the time. I passed out once from drinking too much. Fortunately, I was with my friends, and they made sure I got home safely."

"Did they put you in your bed?"

"Yes, and the next morning I washed all my bedding and took a shower. I had a terrible hangover, but I still forced myself to go through my usual routine until I felt clean again. I don't enjoy being out of control, and I realize drinking or taking pills of any kind does not really solve a problem. It just makes the problem less threatening for a while."

"I'm glad you realize taking pills or drinking too much does not solve a problem.

"I want to talk about your mother again. Why do you hate her so much?"

"She's the reason I am the way I am," I repeated. "According to the studies I've read, a mother has even more influence on a child than the father does. Leslie and I learned at an early age how to please Mom. We just cleaned everything the way she taught us. That's what children do. They learn from their parents by imitating them. I watched Mom use Lysol on door knobs, the kitchen table if someone had put a purse on it, anything she thought was dirty. She cleaned everything excessively."

"Didn't you think there was something strange about the way she cleaned?"

"No, not at the time. I was raised watching her do the cleaning and telling me everything is dirty. I was always willing to please her, and I cleaned the way she showed me. By the time I realized that what I was doing wasn't what I consider normal, it was too late. I already was a freak. Everything bothered me, and I tried to avoid participating in life as much as possible. She is a really good mother who has taken very good care of her three children and her husband. Being a nurse, Mom gave us excellent care whenever we were sick. She has always been there for me, and she has always encouraged me throughout my life. But I just can't or won't get over the anger I feel towards her because I feel she has ruined my life. I became really angry with her during my junior year of high school, and I still am angry. We will talk to each other when necessary, but I try to avoid being with her as much as possible. Leslie doesn't understand why I'm so angry with Mom. I just tell her one day she, too, will probably be angry at Mom."

"I know you said your parents didn't know how to help you, but don't you think they should have taken you to a doctor?"

"Mom took me to the dermatologist during my sophomore year of high school when I was washing my face so much that my skin would flake off. I could rub my chin and dead skin would fall like snow. They didn't realize how bad my condition was at the time. I really don't blame them because we lived in a small town with no counseling centers."

"It must have been difficult for your dad to see you so upset."

"It was difficult for both of my parents, but I think my dad suffered more as he doesn't have OCD. My mom won't admit that she has a problem. I caused arguments between the two of them over my habits, but I would never want them to get a divorce. No matter what Mom has done to me, she is still my mom and even though I hate her, I know deep in my heart that I love her. Funny how parents can do almost anything to their children, and yet the children will accept them for what they are and what they do."

"How did your dad react towards you?"

"My dad used to get mad at me for washing my hands too much and taking long showers. I love him very much, but I'm also afraid of him because I'm worried that I will push him too far. I don't mean that he would physically hurt me, but if he turned against me and no longer loved me, I couldn't take it."

"What would you do if your dad stopped loving you?"

"I would kill myself. My dad is the most important person in my life. He is also the most important person in my twin's life. We have always been 'daddy's girls,' and I would not want to live if he rejected me. I feel terrible because I know I am causing him grief. I just can't stop myself from washing and avoiding things."

"I'm amazed that you have been able to cope for as long as you have."

"I thought about running away my junior year of high school. I had reached a saturation point, and I felt like anything had to be better than living at home with my mom. The only reason I didn't leave was because I didn't know where to go. I knew my parents would find me, and I didn't want to put dad through the embarrassment of everyone in our small town knowing that I had run away. I also knew kids living on the street would eat leftover food from garbage cans. I couldn't imagine living in a dirty environment. It would be worse than what I was living through at home. At least our house was clean, and Mom always took care of us."

"So you stayed and decided when you went to college you would be able to do something about your problem."

"And here I am. You know, since I'm so outgoing, everyone assumes that I'm always happy and nothing bothers me. If they only knew the personal hell I go through every day, they'd be amazed. I'm always in turmoil because I'm a nervous wreck. I feel like a powder keg ready to blow at any second. I'm never relaxed even though I appear to be."

"Well, you have accomplished two big steps: dealing with garbage trucks and using public bathrooms. We will just take one step at a time. You're not going to change 18 years of established behavior quickly."

I continued seeing Dr. Taylor on a regular basis. And life on campus went on as normal – or as normal as possible for someone like me. I enjoyed being with people. As I had told Dr. Taylor, I had a lot of friends of both sexes. But I was only beginning to discover some of the joys of being with guys. During fall quarter, I went to a party and met Dennis. We talked for an hour and then decided to return to his room. He lived in a dorm with two rooms connected by a bathroom. I spent the night with Dennis; I never knew one could become sexually aroused by hugging and kissing.

I did not go home until Thanksgiving break during that freshman year. Mom and I were talking to each other, but it was a tense situation. I was glad when the long holiday weekend ended and I returned to campus. Three weeks later, fall quarter ended, and I returned home for Christmas break.

Soon after I returned to college for winter term, I had a minor concussion. I was getting out of a car, and it started moving before I expected, and I couldn't stop myself. I fell, and my head hit the pavement. I was checked out at the hospital and told I could return to my room after a friend kept watch over me that first night. I was recuperating in Delta, my dorm, which was relatively small with only about a hundred girls. Everyone knew everyone else. All the girls had heard about my concussion, and many dropped into see how I was doing. I was lying in bed all of the time, and if I tried to sit up, everything would start spinning. Lorraine would bring me my food from the dining hall.

I felt well cared for, but I called my sister to stay with me for a while, and she took the bus from Seattle. When Leslie got off the bus in Bellingham, she took a taxi to campus. The driver didn't know which dorm was Delta. All he could tell her was that it was on upper campus. Leslie got out of the taxi carrying a small suitcase and a hair dryer in its own carrying case. The hair dryers of the early 70's had a bonnet that fitted over a head in curlers and were huge and hard to carry.

Leslie couldn't tell which dorm was which as shrubs covered the dorm signs. Eventually she entered Delta. She wandered into the main floor, which was actually on the second floor, right by the mailboxes and TV lounge where about 30 diehard soap-opera fans were watching TV. Leslie, carrying a suitcase, bulky hairdryer, and a blank look on her face, walked into the lounge and said, "Is this Delta?"

"Oh, my God!" Roxanne exclaimed. "Marie is a lot worse than we thought she was. Here she is wandering around the dorm, carrying stuff as if she's going on a trip, and asking if this is her dorm.

"It's okay, Marie. We'll get you back to your room and call the doctor."

"My name isn't Marie. I'm her twin sister, Leslie. Would you take me to her?"

"That's okay, Marie; we'll keep you safe."

Almost everyone from the TV lounge went with Leslie to my room. After navigating several stairs on the same second level, they were getting closer to the first floor. Everyone was yelling what had happened, and by the time they got to the first floor, there were 40 girls tagging along with Leslie. She kept saying over and over again that she was not Marie. When they opened my door and saw me lying in bed, they freaked.

"There really are two of them!" they all screamed.

Leslie let Mom and Dad know what had happened. Dad's reaction was to ask if I was smoking dope. Leslie assured him that I wasn't doing anything illegal, and I would be fine in a few days. One positive outcome from my accident was that Mom and I were talking to each other again without any tension. The concussion shoved my anger aside, and I knew I had missed my close relationship with Mom.

When all of us returned to campus after spring break, we discovered a new member in our dorm: Marla had brought a puppy with her even though animals were not allowed. Two years before a room had to be fumigated because two roommates had had a monkey living in their room.

Linda knew I would be upset with an animal in a room three doors away from me. I wanted to scream at Marla. What the hell was she thinking, bringing a dog to the dorm? I told her it upset me, but I didn't scream. Marla was depressed and had brought the puppy to cheer her up. After talking to Linda, Lorraine and I decided to move from the first floor to the third floor, but I was not pleased with the situation. I was angry that Marla had been so inconsiderate in breaking the rules and that Linda had not enforced them. But I was also angry that my obsession made me so inflexible under such circumstances.

CHAPTER FIVE

I decided during spring quarter that I wanted to attend summer school. Leslie was leaving for Hawaii in June, and I didn't want to go home for the summer. I found a job in the career placement center and lived with a family off campus. The Smiths would let students have free room and board in exchange for doing about four hours of ironing and other light housekeeping chores every week. They had a housekeeper do the heavy work once a week, including cleaning the bathrooms, vacuuming, and scrubbing the floors.

Mrs. Smith interviewed me at her house. They had two large, black cats named Mack and Tofu. I didn't approve of cats being in the house. But I wanted the job, so I said nothing. I convinced myself that since it wasn't my house, I wouldn't let the cats bother me. Working with cats in the house was better than going home and being bored for the summer, as none of my friends were in Quincy anymore.

The Smiths also had a 15-year-old daughter named Teri. Every summer the couple would go to Los Angeles on a buying trip to order more merchandise for their company. During that two-week period, I would also be responsible for chaperoning Teri. I got the job and was excited to move into their beautiful home for the summer as I would have my own bedroom and bathroom.

I continued seeing Dr. Taylor until I quit college after fall quarter of my sophomore year. My disorder did not improve much beyond the two big steps I had accomplished, but it was a big improvement in my life to have someone I could talk to about my mental illness without feeling I was being judged. I never saw Dr. Taylor again. She was my first counselor, and I will always be grateful to her.

Dr. Taylor accomplished two small miracles in my ability to deal with garbage trucks and toilet seats. My heart would still palpitate rapidly when I encountered either situation, but I could at least handle them and appear normal to others. The record keeping she had me do was not very successful as I still washed my hands all the time. It helped me briefly, but I did not change my rituals for any length of time.

I quit college because I thought I would never have a career as a teacher as the job market was glutted with them. Leslie had finished a year of business school and had gone to Hawaii with her good friend Nikki to find work.

Leslie found work in the camera and gift shops located in the huge hotels that catered to the tourists. Nikki worked as a secretary for a plumbing business. I was upset when I quit school; I didn't know what to do with myself. Dad suggested I go to Hawaii and work as it might help me to decide to return to college if I was away from it for a while. I was excited because I had never flown on a plane before, and how could I resist paradise?

I was happy to see Leslie, but I was wondering if she had become a sophisticated city woman who would find me boring. No, Leslie was the same lovable twin I had always known. She insisted that we go to a nightclub in Waikiki the night after I arrived.

"I bought tee-shirts with 'Beach Bum' on them. I want us both to wear red shorts!" Leslie exclaimed.

I was surprised because when we were in the ninth grade, Leslie had insisted that we dress differently. Until then, Mom had always had us in matching outfits, which was fine by me. But Leslie wanted to be thought of as an individual. Mom was not pleased, but Dad agreed with Leslie. At Leslie's insistence, we hadn't dressed alike since early high school, and now she wanted us to dress as twins.

We arrived at the nightclub Captain Nemo's, and the bouncer said, "You can't come in here with shorts on."

"Leslie, I asked you before we left if it'd be all right to wear shorts."

She just stood there looking forlorn. "I'm sorry. I thought they'd let us in."

The bouncer, who had heard us talking, smiled and said, "Beach bums. Well, I'm not supposed to let you in, but I will this time. But next time wear long pants or dresses.

We thanked him profusely. I had never been to a nightclub as the drinking age in Washington State was 21. In Hawaii, one could enter a bar at 18. Having the lower drinking age made sense to me because the islands had a huge military population with hundreds of servicemen who were under 21.

To enter the nightclub, we walked down steps into a scene resembling a submarine. There were fish tanks everywhere that blended into the theme of the nightclub. I was very excited, and so was Leslie. We each order a chi chi. A guy in the Navy named Bob asked me to dance. I danced with him until we left. Leslie lived halfway between Honolulu and Waikiki, so we had walked to the nightclub. Neither Leslie nor Nikki had a car while living in Hawaii because of the expense and limited parking spaces. Besides, they were dating guys who had cars. On the way home from the club, we walked along the beach. Bob swirled me into his arms and walked into the ocean. I thought it was so romantic; I wasn't even bothered about my new sandals getting soaked. The three of us went back to the apartment. Nikki was home with her boy friend, and the five of us sat and talked for two hours. Bob left, saying he would call me.

I took two weeks off to have a vacation before I started looking for work. Much of that time, I sat in the apartment waiting for Bob to call. He finally did, but it was six weeks later. I could have kicked myself for all the time I wasted not going to the beach because I was sitting and waiting for the phone to ring. Never again did I wait for the phone. If someone wanted to call me, I would eventually be home and he would reach me.

Since Leslie and Nikki were already roommates and had no extra room, Leslie arranged for me to move in with Carolyn. She was 26 and from Portland, Oregon. I liked her as she was the big sister I had never had. She helped me pick a dress to wear and did my hair for interviews. I started working as a secretary at Pioneer Federal Savings and Loan in the Fort Street office of downtown Honolulu. I felt lucky to get the position as it was in a beautiful office in the area known as the financial plaza of the Pacific. I was in charge of safe-deposit boxes, taking care of the Xerox machine, and other duties. Working in a savings and loan required obtaining state identification and being bonded. Anyone working in a bank had to be fingerprinted with a photo identification attached to the document.

On the second day of work during my lunch break, I walked over to the state offices to be bonded. Coming from a small town, I was not prepared for some of the events I would see in a large city. I was standing in line waiting for my picture to be processed when the clerk asked the two women standing next to me their addresses. At least I thought they were two women until one of them answered the clerk's question in a deep, masculine voice. I observed them closer and was shocked to see they were men dressed as women. They both had hairy legs and were standing with their legs wide apart. They did not have any feminine characteristics. I had heard of transvestites and seen some of them on the streets of Honolulu, but I had never been right next to them. Living in a big city was a very educational experience for a girl coming from a farming community in the middle of Washington State.

While I was working at the savings and loan, I vividly remember one woman who wanted to open a safe-deposit box. One day an Air Force colonel's wife came in who looked like the Disney character Cruella De Vil. A hair piece swept her hair up a half foot above her head, and she was smoking a cigarette on a long holder. She looked at me as if I were nothing and said, "I would like to open a safe-deposit box."

I took out the necessary forms and asked her where she lived.

She puffed on her cigarette and said, "Aiea."

"How do you spell that?"

Putting her hands on her hips, she scoffed, "Didn't they teach you anything in school?"

By this time I wanted to punch her in the face, but I reminded myself of the adage that the customer is always right. I was glad I had given her an appropriate name in my thoughts as she was certainly living up to the image.

I looked straight at her and replied, "I'm sorry, madam, but I'm from Washington. I've been in the islands for only three weeks. I don't even know how to pronounce Hawaiian words let alone spell most of them.

As soon as Cruella De Vil realized I was not a native, her attitude changed. This was not the first time I had experience misplaced prejudice. When I was little, our new neighbor had yelled at her daughter for playing tag with Leslie and me. She had been furious to see her little blonde girl having fun with children she thought were Mexican. She found out later we were the daughters of her husband's new employer. Only years later did she reveal this to my mom.

And here I was, once again, being taken for being something I was not. I had a tan, and I wore my dark hair long and straight, which made me look as much native Hawaiian as Mexican. I was disgusted that Cruella De Vil was acting nice to me because she now knew I wasn't a native.

With a shocked look on her face, she said, "Aiea is spelled a, i, e, a. There are twelve letters in the Hawaiian alphabet, and it is common for vowels to be used without consonants."

I continued processing her request and was glad when she left. My roommate, Carolyn, sometimes had the opposite reaction. She was blonde and felt hostility from natives who didn't like her because she was not a native. One of my high school classmates was living in Honolulu. He informed me what the different races thought of each other. I felt sorry that mankind had such difficulty seeing beneath the surface and appreciating all people for who they are.

My OCD didn't bother me to any extent when I lived in Hawaii as I was able to relax and adapt to the "hang loose" philosophy. I introduced Nikki to Gary, a friend of Bob's, who was also in the Navy. Years later, Nikki married Gary. Leslie was a bridesmaid, and I attended the guest book. They have been married for more than 30 years and have three children. My husband Doug and I now live within five miles of their home.

I was happy in Hawaii, but I talked about Mom and Dad all the time. My roommate, Carolyn, said I was making Leslie homesick. I didn't believe her. Five months after

I had arrived, Leslie told me she was homesick and wanted to go home.

"What? I just got here, and now you want to leave!"

Leslie left about three weeks later, and I became an emotional wreck. I started jamming food in my mouth on my work breaks and ballooned up to 130 pounds. I gave the savings and loan two weeks notice that I was quitting. I should have asked for a leave of absence as I decided I didn't really want to go home, but it was too late. I was crying constantly when I wasn't working.

CHAPTER SIX

When I got home, Mom took me to the doctor. I had a nervous breakdown, but the doctor was too polite to use those words. He assured me I would be all right after I calmed down. I decided to go back to college only two weeks before the start of fall quarter. At the last minute my friend Diane, who I had expected to be with me, decided to wait until winter quarter to start college again. I had been assigned to a freshman dorm with three hundred screaming teenagers. I was so upset I couldn't unpack. I panicked. I felt so sorry for Mom because she spent five hours driving me to campus, and then I just had her turn around and take me home again. I was upset for three months and lost all the weight I had gained. Mom and Dad were very patient with me.

I had a great time when I finally returned to campus. I studied, went to parties, and dated. My OCD was always with me, but I was able to cope. I couldn't believe it when one of my roommates put her shoes on the kitchen counter and cleaned them with the dish rag. After she left for class, I took a hanger to pick up the dish rag and put it in the laundry.

During my junior year, three roommates and I decided to have a party with each of us inviting 15 people for a total of 60. We invited everyone in our four-plex; we didn't want anyone calling the police, complaining we were disturbing the peace. About 80 came; some of them we didn't know. The party was fun, but the apartment was a disaster. The kitchen floor had a thick coating of sticky, dried beer, and the rugs and furniture smelled of stale beer. We cleaned as well as we could. I don't know how I ever allowed myself to have a party where I lived. I was going through a period where I ignored my OCD when I didn't want to be bothered with my habits. I was not seeing anyone professionally as Dr. Taylor had left the university. I just managed to survive, but I still took long showers and avoided objects and situations that had always bothered me.

In the summer of 1974, Leslie and I went on a six-week bus tour of Europe, which included sixteen countries. Going to Europe was both exciting and exasperating for someone with OCD.

In Paris we rolled down the sloping lawns surrounding the Eiffel Tower. After we got to the bottom, we walked back to the top and rolled down again. I felt good to be so carefree, and I didn't even care that I was on the ground. Europe wasn't as clean as America, so I relaxed and decided I didn't care.

We stayed at a new hotel in Paris. I opened the bathroom door and thought what a dumb toilet. Karen, a nurse on our trip, was pounding on our door. We let her in and she explained that it was a bidet. I had never seen one before except in pictures, but I was glad another door in the room led to standard bathroom facilities.

Our tour took us on the "other" side of the Berlin Wall, which was still a formidable barrier then. The tour guide instructed us not to take pictures of East German military installations. Jean, one of our traveling companions, heard those instructions, but she was cavalier about rules and obeyed only those she wanted to. She was sitting in the back of the bus snapping one picture after another. I couldn't contain myself, and I grabbed her camera. I wanted to stomp on it until it was broken, but instead, shaking so hard I could barely talk. I screamed at her, "Do you want us all to land in jail?" Jean wasn't apologetic, but she did stop taking pictures.

In 1974 there were three checkpoints in and out of East Berlin. We were at Checkpoint Charlie, waiting to enter. A section of no man's land separated the East from the West. Two guards with machine guns and German shepherds boarded our bus. Each passport was checked twice. Leslie and I, being identical twins, had our passports checked with our faces three times each. But the guards were young and handsome, we were young and cute, and a smile is the universal language. I finally smiled at them and said, "Yes, there are really two of us." I don't know if they understood English, but I'm sure they understood what I meant.

Before the bus was allowed to leave, a huge mirror was rolled under the bus to be sure no one was tied up under the frame of the bus, trying to escape. A man had once got his wife out by jacking his car up and strapping her underneath. He published an article about his experience; now every vehicle had to be checked. East Berlin was gray, grim, and depressing. People on the street looked at us through the bus windows, and I knew they were thinking those people are free. It was sobering to know what freedom really represents.

As we continued towards southern Europe, two soldiers rode with us for two hundred miles. It was nerve wracking to see them in the back of the bus with guns over their shoulders, but they were playing cards with some of the group and seemed happy. One rest stop in Yugoslavia was filthy; the bathrooms were backed up with raw sewage ankle deep. Some of the women went anyway, but I stayed on the bus. An hour later our bus had a flat tire. While we were waiting for the tire to be changed, a group of us went into the foothills and relieved ourselves behind trees. Nature is much cleaner than most public bathrooms.

I don't know how we managed to cope for six weeks, but we did. We had relaxed a little in the foreign environments and were able not to worry about every little thing. Still, when it was time to leave Europe, Leslie and I were relieved. We were glad to be returning to our regular surroundings where we would felt cleaner. Once at home, we thoroughly sprayed our suitcases with Lysol.

In 1975 I was a camp counselor at Lake Wenatchee. Our director, Susan, was pretty lax with the staff. After we put our campers to bed at night, she let us drive three miles to Cougar Inn to party. When a boy from the YMCA camp across the lake drowned on a hike, Susan finally insisted we obey the rules. Most parents wouldn't have sent their children to camp if they had had any idea of the lack of supervision. I was three years older than most of the other counselors, and I felt more responsible for the campers. Most of the counselors would take their groups to the lake and leave them with one lifeguard. The counselors were supposed to stay there, but they went to the staff room to play cards and gossip. That changed after the drowning, and Susan insisted we stay with the campers.

The camp had indoor plumbing for counselors, but I was appalled because there were mouse droppings everywhere, including on the bars of soap. The campers had to use outhouses. At least they had sinks and showers available. I had signed a contract to be a counselor for six weeks; I wasn't sure if I could keep my promise when I saw the condition of the camp. For the first two days, I used the bathroom in the medical facilities until I was able to calm down enough to use the regular facilities. I survived six weeks, but I decided I would never be a camp counselor again as the outdoors created too many terrifying situations for me. One girl had to have a tick removed from her hair. Another one almost died because of a wasp sting.

When I returned from camp, I hosed out my car with Lysol because there were mouse droppings in the trunk. At least the mice hadn't been able to enter the car itself, but I still felt everything was contaminated. I took my clothes to a local Laundromat because I didn't want to use the washing machine at our apartment. I washed several loads at once, pouring Lysol into the water. It took me several weeks to feel completely clean again.

After spending two more quarters at college, I quit again. I was distraught. Leslie was working in Wenatchee at a bank, and I decided I would live with her. Mom and Dad convinced me to go to the local community college even though I knew it would be like high school after attending the university. I enrolled in business education classes to become a secretary. I finished a secretarial program at the community college and started working. I hated my job, and Dad was the one who convinced me I would never be happy until I finished my degree. I had one more year left, and I didn't want to be far from home. I went to Central Washington University, which is 50 miles from Quincy.

Finally in the spring of 1977, I graduated with degrees in Business Education and English.

CHAPTER SEVEN

I applied for teaching positions to ten school districts, believing if I couldn't get a full-time job where I wanted to be located, I would substitute teach in a district until I could get hired. Eastmont Junior High School in East Wenatchee in eastern Washington needed a combination English and typing teacher. I was thrilled when I received the call I had been hired. There were 13 teaching positions opened in the entire district for the school year 1977-1978, and there were 600 applicants. Dad and Mom were proud of me, and they were also relieved I had finally found my niche after quitting college twice.

By the time I started teaching at 24, I usually wouldn't go anywhere on the weekend so I could avoid getting into situations that might make me feel contaminated. I avoided going on dates, refused to go to friends' houses if they had animals, and became a stay at home person. I developed agoraphobia, and for me to have to go back out into the world on a Monday morning was very stressful.

Teaching in junior high presented its own special challenges. In the beginning, I was 24, only ten years older than my students. It is hard to keep a strict professional distance when one is young and enjoys being with students. In my first two years, the students seemed more like younger brothers and sisters to me. My principal, Harry, knew I was having a difficult time, but he told me he would rather see me too attached to the students than too distant. Harry told me, "As you grow older, you'll notice the generation gap."

It happened soon enough. One day the janitor said, "Congratulations, you're finally a member of this staff."

I looked at him, wondering what he meant.

Tom replied, "I don't consider a new teacher part of the school until his or her name appears in the bathrooms. Graffiti in the boys' bathroom says you're a bitch. You've made it, Marie."

How does one respond to such a statement? At least he had cleaned the words off, and I thanked him for that.

Other incidents were more bothersome. Once early in my teaching career, I came into my English classroom, and the students were already there. The bell hadn't rung yet. Lying on the floor three feet from my desk was a clean sanitary napkin. I tried not to stare at it; I ignored it as best I could and taught class. After the students left, I had the janitor get rid of it.

Another time someone had put a clean condom on my desk. I called the office, and Harry came to my room. I told him what had happened. He brought the wastebasket over to my desk and used the stapler to push the condom into the wastebasket. I didn't say anything to the students, and neither did he. Sometimes it is best to ignore what the students do as they feel they have won if a teacher becomes upset. Other times, we need to respond. The home economics teacher once caught three boys throwing condoms full of water around the cooking lab. She sent them to the office so she could continue teaching class.

Another time, I was in the gym with a group of teachers when Harry asked me to check the girls' shower stalls in the locker room as someone had spread blood over the tile. "I'm sorry to ask you to do this, Marie, but I can't go into the girls' locker room."

Harry didn't know about my OCD at the time, and I wasn't about to tell him. My face dropped, and I looked sick, but I went to check. Fortunately, the janitor had already cleaned the tile.

As time went on, my OCD became worse. Different people and situations started bothering me more and more; I could hardly function. I would avoid walking up and down the aisles of students because I didn't want to become contaminated by someone who wasn't wearing clean clothes. If a student was sitting with his legs crossed, I didn't want to walk by him because I was afraid to get near the bottom of his shoe. All I could think of was my mom saying over and over again "the floor is dirty." Shoes are on the floor; therefore, they are dirty. I felt like Howard Hughes who was known to isolate himself from everyone.

I knew I needed to get professional help again so I could function more normally and calmly in my job. I started seeing a psychologist named Dr. Brizee. He was very understanding and tried to help me, but he couldn't prescribe medications. Dr. Brizee could ask my physician to write out prescriptions, but I wanted to see a psychiatrist so I didn't have to bother my regular physician.

Fortunately, I found Dr. Stevens who had his practice in the Wenatchee Valley Clinic. I had not been in treatment, except for seeing Dr. Brizee for a short time, since the fall of 1972 when I had last consulted with Dr. Taylor as a sophomore in college. I started therapy with Dr. Stevens in January 1980. He was a very serious man who tried to help me, but I was not a good patient. He prescribed Valium and noted on my chart that I was less anxious and tense with the medication. He helped me by working on tension reduction and psychotherapy. In April of 1980, Dr. Stevens wrote that I was "quite optimistic and [was] getting out of [the] house and functioning at a much higher level." He prescribed different medications such as Imipramine and Lomotil. Dr. Stevens reminded me in May 1980 that I was still not taking Imipramine, and I was not doing the tension reduction techniques he had taught me. I knew I was not doing well and becoming less functional.

CHAPTER EIGHT

The only reason I went to the hospital and was admitted to the psychiatric ward in 1980 was to keep from losing my teaching position. I had been teaching for only three years, and I was coping as best I could with my OCD and all that the job required. I made the mistake of telling a teacher friend named Sherry about my problem. I told her how I didn't want to touch papers students handed in because they had been on the floor. This was told in confidence, but she thought she was doing me a favor by telling our principal Harry about it. Harry started observing me more. I was very nervous as I knew he was outside my classroom making sure I was going up and down the aisles helping students and not being immobile behind my desk. I knew he knew I was being watched, but there were many times when Harry was near, and I pretended he wasn't there.

I realized that I needed to do something drastic if I was going to continue to function and keep my career. I decided to see another psychiatrist while I was finishing my Master's program at Central Washington University in Ellensburg. In June of 1980 I started sessions with Dr. Montgomery, a psychiatrist in Yakima, Washington, which is 30 miles from the university I was attending. I went for sessions twice a week. Dr. Montgomery was proficient and thorough. He informed me my OCD was not as extreme as some of the patients he had worked with in the past. He wanted me to cut in half the number of times I washed my hands.

"I think you can do this on your own, Marie, but if you do not succeed, I want you to be admitted to Yakima Valley Memorial Hospital where we can monitor your behavior and put you through a program designed to help you with your disorder. On a scale of one to ten with ten being the worst, I would say that you are a three in your ability to deal with OCD."

I tried to reduce how often I washed my hands, but I was not successful. Therefore, I arranged to commit myself to the psychiatric ward for two weeks after I finished summer school in 1980. I was happy because I had just completed my Master's Degree, and I still had three weeks before I started teaching again. I drove to the hospital by myself as I did not want my family around the dirty environment of the hospital. I took old clothes, so I could throw them away after I left the facility if I felt they were too dirty to wash. I didn't even bother with a suitcase. The idea of getting it dirty was unacceptable to me so I arrived at the hospital with my clothes in a sack. After checking in at the admissions desk, I was escorted to the top floor where the ward was located. Since I had never been in a psychiatric ward before, everything was new to me. I didn't know at the time that many psychiatric wards are separated into two sections. The patients that were a threat to themselves and others were put in the ward that was more secure. The hospital I entered had one ward for everyone, and I was scared to be with people who heard voices, screamed, and walked around looking or being crazy. The most extreme patients were taken to the state hospital for the mentally ill.

The first observation I remembered was that the ward was locked. A key was used by a staff member to operate the elevator. I felt trapped, and I had committed myself voluntarily. What was I thinking? Why would I do this to myself? The answer was I desperately wanted to function again on a normal level; I was willing to try anything. The nurse took me to my room, so I could put my sack of clothes there. I felt dumb carrying a sack instead of a suitcase, but the thought of anything being taken home besides a sack I could throw away was out of the question.

I stared through the rain-spattered window of my hospital room knowing that I would never be cured or completely free of my problem. I asked myself a question that had been haunting me for years. Did I really want to get better? OCD provided a perfect excuse for me not to do anything I didn't want to do. My mental illness had become a crutch for me, and I could always use my disorder to get attention and to avoid unpleasant or difficult situations. I knew I wasn't being honest with myself when I turned away from life and my problems. But I found it easier to ignore them for short periods of time by drifting into an imaginary world where I dreamed.

The nurse interrupted my thoughts by telling me about the rules of the ward. Another staff member showed me the rest of the psychiatric wing. I remember her pointing out the locked room for uncontrollable patients. I had no intention of being put in that room with a straight jacket on me.

Shortly after I arrived, it was time for dinner. The food was brought in on a rolling cart with each patient's food on a separate tray. Surprisingly, the dinner tasted good to me, but I have never been a fussy eater. Since there wasn't a separate dining area, all patients ate in the recreation room. One of the most depressing times of my life was sitting there trying to eat when I was so upset. Everyone else looked either sad, angry, depressed, or a combination of all these emotions. I am usually a very outgoing person who is not afraid to start a conversation with people. I sat there with my head down and forced myself to eat. The rest of the evening I had free, and I watched some television in the lounge area. I was bored, so I went to bed early.

Early the next morning my psychiatrist, Dr. Montgomery, embarrassed me when he came into my room with two male counselors at about seven o'clock. I was still in bed, but he told me to stay there.

"Good morning, Marie. This is Doug and Rick, the two counselors who will be working with you. They are both college graduates, working on their Master's Degree in psychology."

Why do they both have to be young and good looking? I thought as Dr. Montgomery started explaining about the behavior modification program. Dr. Montgomery's words interrupted my thoughts as I focused on what he was saying.

"First of all, every morning you will be timed for the number of minutes it takes you to shower. We will start you with a ten minute shower."

"Ten minute shower! I'll never get clean in just ten minutes. It usually takes me anywhere from 30 to 60 minutes to feel clean."

"Well, you will have to get used to it because everyday you will be given less time to take a shower until you are down to five minutes. Doug will have a stopwatch and will be sitting just outside the bathroom door, timing your showers."

Why can't a woman staff member do this? I wanted to protest loudly, but I kept my thoughts to myself as I realized there wasn't much room for privacy in a hospital.

Dr. Montgomery continued telling my counselors and me what my daily schedule would include. "After you shower and eat breakfast, you will start on your behavior modification program to help you eliminate compulsive activities. Doug will help you make a list of the ten worst activities that make you feel contaminated. Then you will start working on the least bothersome one with the idea that you will eventually get through the entire list and eliminate the need to wash your hands after each of the ten activities. This method is known as systematic desensitization."

I don't want to do this. I don't want to make a list, and I don't want to do anything I consider dirty. I know what you are doing. I know behavior modification is a treatment to help the patient modify his behavior until identified behaviors eventually become extinct.

After breakfast, Doug handed me a towel and sat outside the bathroom inside my hospital room to time my shower. *This is ridiculous.* At the end of ten minutes, he told me to turn off the water. Fortunately, he left the room while I got dressed. Then we went to the lounge and ate breakfast. Doug told me to make a list of ten things I would not do or found difficult to do because I considered them dirty and rank them from the least threatening to the most threatening. It wasn't easy to keep the list to only ten instances as there were so many things that bothered me. It took me an hour to come up with the following list:

1. Sitting close to a wastebasket or walking by anything that I think is dirty
2. Touching a person who is not clean
3. Doing laundry (the clothes are dirty, so they make me dirty)
4. Housekeeping (vacuuming, dusting, cleaning the bathroom, etc.)
5. Sitting on the ground, floor, or sidewalk
6. Not being able to wash my hands immediately when I feel contaminated

7. Picking up something from the floor or ground
8. Being around animals or having to touch animals
9. Changing a baby's diaper
10. Touching or taking out garbage

"Now that you've finished the list," said Doug, "we're going to start on the first one. Dr. Montgomery told me we are to start out slow. Let's go sit somewhere in the lounge that is far from the wastebasket. Then we'll walk over and sit closer to it and then still nearer until you are sitting in a chair that is right next to it. We'll also walk by it several times."

"I don't want people knowing why I'm here. I don't want them seeing us do all this."

"I know what you must be feeling. We'll go into a part of the lounge that's usually locked. No one will be there except us. And listen, Marie, the other patients will know nothing about what's going on unless you tell them about it. Does that make you feel better?"

I indicated to Doug I understood, and we spent an hour going through step one. I felt quite comfortable sitting next to the wastebasket by the end of the hour. Doug told me Dr. Montgomery had informed him it made me extremely nervous to walk around outside because of what I might encounter so he suggested we go outside and walk around the hospital grounds.

"I don't want to because there are items outside that bother me. I don't want to walk by any trash cans, dumpsters, manhole covers, or drainage areas for storm water."

"Now, Marie, you know this is part of your treatment. We'll walk slowly, and you gradually try to increase the time you are near things you find contaminating."

We walked around the hospital talking about college. I found out Doug had graduated from the same university that I had. He needed to work for a while in order to start graduate school. Eventually he wanted to be a psychologist with his own office.

Doug was two years younger than I was, and I was surprised he was really interested in my problem.

"I get so tired of taking care of drunks or people that have been ordered here by the court. We get many alcoholics who are trying to dry out and put their shattered lives back together. I know they need help too, but you're the first patient I have worked with that has an interesting illness. I'm tired of talking to people who are messed up in their heads because of alcohol and drugs. You're a wonderful change over most of the cases I've been given. It's a challenge to spend time with someone who came here on a voluntary basis to work through a behavior modification program; this treatment is completely different from anything I have done."

I was shocked that my counselor would tell me this, but I sensed his frustration with his assignments in the psychiatric ward.

"Don't tell anyone I told you how I feel."

"Don't worry, Doug; I'll keep it to myself."

I begin to feel a bond with him as we now shared a secret. Rick, the other counselor, was supposed to work with me, too, but because he was busy with other patients, Doug spent more time with me. We walked close to dumpsters and grates, and I started backing off. Doug wouldn't let me avoid things. "You know this is on your list, and you have to get through the ten items on it before you're released."

"That isn't true since I entered the hospital voluntarily."

"You know what I mean, Marie. If you're going to get better, you'll have to force yourself to do activities you want to avoid."

Since I knew he was right, I didn't reply. We kept walking closer and closer to the dumpsters, but we didn't touch them. I was very apprehensive and quiet.

The next morning Dr. Montgomery looked at my chart. "Well, Marie, I see you washed your hands several times yesterday. Today we are going to cut down on the number of times you wash. You will not be allowed to wash every time you feel your hands are contaminated. Sometimes you will have to wait five minutes after you feel the need to wash your hands before you will be allowed to wash them. Also, see if you can cut your shower down to seven minutes this morning. I see you progressed with sitting by the wastebasket. I am pleased with the ten activities you listed, and today I want you to work on numbers two, three, and four."

The routine of the day before started all over again. I took an eight minute shower although I felt it was not long enough to get really clean. Doug recorded the time on my chart. We went through step one again to reinforce sitting by the wastebasket.

"Now, Marie, number two is 'touching a person who is not clean.'"

"Yes, I don't want to get near anyone who is not wearing clean clothes and needs a bath. If I have to touch the person, I feel that I've become contaminated as I relate everything. For instance, if you touched the floor and then touched me, I would feel unclean. Or if you threw something in the trash can and touched it, then your hand would be contaminated by the can. But if you tossed the item out without touching the trash can, then I'd think your hand wasn't dirty – as long as you hadn't gotten too near it. This is crazy, but I can't help the way I relate to objects. It causes me so much stress that most of the time I don't want to be here."

"What do you mean 'here'?"

"Here in this world. I wish I were dead so I wouldn't have to deal with any of this anymore. I'm so tired of living with OCD day after day!"

Stunned by my revelation, Doug stared at me. "We'll help you through this," he offered. "There are so many reasons to go on living. Let's find something for me to touch, and then you'll have to touch my hand afterwards. We'll start with something you don't consider very dirty. Here's a clean wastebasket that has a clean plastic sack around the rim; I'm going to throw some tissue in it. Now touch my hand."

I didn't want to touch his hand, and I felt we were playing a silly game that wouldn't help me at all. To keep the therapy going, I touched his hand. We did this several times using separate clean pieces of tissue each time. "Now, Marie, I'm going to throw the tissue away, but this time I'm going to touch the wastebasket and then you'll hold my hand."

"No! I won't do it!" I ran to the far corner of the room.

"Come on, Marie. You've got to go through the steps. This is all a natural progression, and the idea is to make these behaviors extinct."

"Don't you think I realize that? I know what's going on. By exposing me to objects, each one a bit dirtier than the previous one, you're trying to get me used to the really dirty ones. The idea is to get me so that any contaminated object doesn't bother me at all. The technical term is desensitization with the end result being extinction of the unwanted behaviors. I know why Dr. Montgomery is using the list of activities, too. It's a hierarchy that he hopes will eventually disappear. I just finished my Master's Degree in Education, but I took several classes in psychology as an undergraduate. I know exactly what is taking place.

"I am depressed, and I want to take a nap."

"Marie, it's only 10:30 in the morning. You didn't come here to take naps. Nurse Jensen told me that you had taken a two hour nap yesterday afternoon. She had come in to give you a Valium, and there you were still sleeping. You went to bed the night before at eight. They keep track of everything you do. Even though she was not on duty when you arrived, it was recorded on your chart when you went to bed."

"I feel like an experimental study with these charts," I replied sarcastically. "Just leave me alone."

"You know that's a bad attitude to take. We're all trying to help you, and you have to be willing to cooperate with us. You may know all the correct terms and understand exactly what we are doing, but that doesn't mean you are going to solve this all by yourself. You wouldn't be here if you really felt that way. Quit being stubborn, and let's continue the therapy. I'm going to touch the wastebasket, just the rim, and then I want you to touch my hand. Here we go. Now touch my hand."

Very slowly I reached out to touch Doug's hand. At the last second, I pulled my hand away and retreated. After seeing the look in Doug's eyes, I came back to him and after 30 seconds I touched his hand. I instantly felt contaminated."

"Now, I want you to hold my hand, not just touch it."

"Do I have to do this?"

"Yes, Marie, if you want to get past step two."

I held his hand even though I wanted to take a shower. Next, Doug wanted to do step three. "Why do you consider laundry dirty? How does it make you dirty to handle it?"

"The laundry *is* dirty. That's why we have to wash it – to get it clean. So when I touch it to put it in the washer; I get contaminated from it. I want to take a shower immediately before I touch it again when it is through being washed and is clean. If I touch the clean laundry while I still feel contaminated, then the clean laundry is dirty again."

Doug had me wash some laundry, and I was able to get through the step because I didn't think the laundry was very dirty. I already felt contaminated being in a hospital. People think a hospital is sterile, but it is one of the most germ infested environments. Doctors and nurses do not wash their hands enough; therefore, they help spread infection. I felt crummy anyway, so doing laundry didn't bother me as much as it would have if I'd been in my clean environment at home. In fact, I'm able to adapt to situations better when I am away from home because I don't feel as if I am contaminating my clean home. I actually relax when I'm on vacation, and I sometimes think I should spend my whole life traveling. I know it's not realistic. I'd get tired of being gone all the time, plus the expense would be astronomical. Even then, I'd still have to travel only to clean places that have indoor plumbing and all the amenities of the civilized world.

Next, I did some vacuuming and dusting, which made me feel unclean because of the dust I could smell in my nose and on my clothes. At least I made it through the three steps. After lunch, I took another nap. Sleep was the only time I could get away from OCD. The rest of the day was a continuation of the first four steps.

The next day I took a seven-minute shower, ate breakfast, and started on the day's schedule. Step five involved sitting on the ground, floor, sidewalk, and anything else that made me feel contaminated. It was a beautiful day, and Doug suggested we go to the park across the street and sit on the lawn. I was not willing to do this, but we went anyway. When we got to the park, Doug immediately sat down on the lawn. I just stood there.

"What are you doing, Marie?"

"Nothing, I'm just standing here, making sure there's nothing on the grass that's going to bother me like animal waste."

"Why don't you finish looking and then sit down beside me?"

"Just give me time. I don't like to sit on the floor or ground anywhere. All I can remember from the time I could remember anything was that the floor is dirty. Mom always says, 'Don't touch the floor or sit on it.'"

I gradually lowered myself to the ground and sat down. I already felt dirty from sitting, so I just stretched out on the lawn. Having more of my body touch the ground wouldn't make any difference; I'd still feel compelled to wash myself thoroughly afterward. For now I felt great to lie on the grass as I hadn't done it for years. I actually started to relax. Again, if I'm in a situation where I don't feel clean, I can adapt for the moment. But I will still want to take a shower before I go back to my clean environment. I knew at the hospital I wouldn't be able to take another shower until tomorrow morning, but I felt all right as I wasn't at my home.

"What are you thinking about, Marie?"

"I was thinking about how nice it is to do something that is so natural and how I used to do this as a kid all the time. I'm actually doing step six as I want to wash my hands right now, but I can't. You know, I wonder if Dr. Montgomery would allow me to go out at night. Like on a date. I never go out with guys anymore because I am afraid they'll find out what I'm really like."

"Hey, that might be a good idea. I'll ask him about it. Maybe you could go see a movie with me downtown."

"Do you mind going out with me? I'm your patient so it wouldn't be a real date; you don't have to feel obligated to take me anywhere."

"No," Doug said, "I would be interested to see how you'd reacted to different situations outside the controlled hospital environment. It'd be fascinating to see your reactions. I'll ask him this afternoon when he comes in to see you. We should start working more on step six which is not being able to wash your hands immediately after you feel unclean. I mean, you've already sat around without being able to wash your hands right away when you felt dirty. Go pick up that rock over there and bring it to me."

I gave Doug the rock, and we started to walk back to the hospital. Doug took out his wallet and dropped it on the street.

"Pick up my wallet for me."

Even though it bothered me, I grabbed his wallet from the street, being careful to not touch the pavement.

I didn't see Doug the rest of the day. Rick worked with me, instead, which was unusual since Doug seemed to be my primary counselor there. I wondered what was going on with Doug. I got my answer the next day. Doug saw me in the morning, and he looked furious. I was afraid to talk to him.

"Hey, Marie, let's go and sit in the other room, so I can tell you about yesterday afternoon. I told the doctor about your idea of going to a movie, and that I had volunteered to take you to get you out into the real world. I mentioned I thought it'd be good for you to go on a pretend date. He became uptight, and though he didn't actually say it, I'm sure he thought we were becoming involved with each other. It made me angry! He acted as if I couldn't take you on a date and be professional about it. Like I was going to try and get romantic with you or something. It just shows how much faith he has in me as your counselor. Dr. Montgomery informed me that it would be better if someone else took over your treatment. I just wanted you to know, so you wouldn't think I was ignoring you or that you had done something wrong."

I was stunned. I thanked Doug for telling me. I felt bad I had even suggested going on a date. I was mad at Dr. Montgomery because I felt he didn't trust me either. I knew I shouldn't get angry as it would affect my treatment. Dr. Montgomery probably thought it would detract from my main purpose if I went outside the hospital. He must have his reasons, and I didn't think I should stay mad at my psychiatrist.

Dr. Montgomery arrived at 10 a.m. and did not explain his decision to switch counselors. He asked me how my treatment was progressing and pretended nothing was different. He told me that Rick, the other counselor, would continue working with me.

I looked at him with a question in my eyes, but Dr. Montgomery kept talking about my behavioral modification program and my progress.

"How did you do when you couldn't wash your hands every time you wanted to? What did you feel when you had to wait five minutes to wash?"

"It was terrible; I hated it. I was upset and very nervous. I felt unclean, and I couldn't wait to feel clean again."

"Okay, Marie, calm down. Just remember what we're trying to accomplish here. I'm sorry I didn't get in to see you the last two afternoons. I'll try and come in this afternoon. I've been talking to Doug about your progress. He told me he's pleased with your results although you resisted him at times."

"Yeah, I know," I replied meekly. I was sick of the routine, the hospital, and everything else dealing with my illness. I just wanted to go home and hide from the world.

One of the nurses brought a pet rabbit to the ward, so I could get through step eight, which involved touching animals. I also fed some ducks at a park when we went there for a picnic.

"It's time to start working on step nine which is changing a baby's diaper. I'll have Rick take you to pediatrics."

"I think I can handle a wet diaper, but not a dirty diaper. It makes me want to throw up. I don't want to be around babies because they stink, and they are always crawling on the floor."

"Well, let's just wait and see how you do," Dr. Montgomery replied. "Also, I want you to do step ten which is touching and taking out garbage. Rick will gradually expose you to garbage cans. There's a big dumpster in the rear of the hospital. We'll have you take out some bags of garbage this afternoon."

I dreaded the thought of getting near a dumpster as much as I dreaded being near a baby. All I could think of was that if I got through these last two steps, I could go home to my safe environment. Changing a dirty diaper bothered me more than taking out garbage. I was able to change a wet diaper, but I backed away from changing a soiled one as I started to gag and get dizzy. I wasn't forced to continue step nine.

Rick didn't mention anything about what had happened with Doug. I thought I should also act as if nothing were different.

"Let's start on step ten, which is touching or taking out garbage."

"Oh, yuk, I don't want to touch garbage cans; they're grotesque!"

"Garbage cans can be grotesque, but you have to try and get through the step. We'll start with a garbage can that looks clean and then find one that's grimy. Later on, I'll have you put some garbage in a dumpster," said Rick.

We slowly approached a garbage can on the sidewalk. I turned around and started to walk in the opposite direction.

"Come back here, Marie. You're just trying to avoid what you need to accomplish. Look, I'll touch the garbage can, and then I'll touch your hand. Then I want you to touch the garbage can."

"I don't want to touch your hand or the garbage can. It's dirty, and I'll feel so contaminated."

"I know, Marie, but you've got to force yourself to go through these steps if you want to get better. How are you supposed to cope with situations if you don't expose yourself to them?"

I looked at Rick as if he were an ogre. I walked back towards him, and he touched the garbage can and then tried to touch my hand. I backed up and stood there with a sour look on my face.

"Hold my hand, Marie."

Somehow I managed to hold his hand even though I felt as if I were going to throw up. Next he gave me two bags of garbage to put in the dumpster. I felt so contaminated by then that I just did it to get through the final step.

"How do you cope with your dad being a dairy farmer if human or animal waste bothers you so much?" inquired Dr. Montgomery.

"Oh, my Dad quit being a dairy farmer before I was born. I think if he had stayed with dairy farming, I would really have had a problem with even staying at home when I was in high school. Thank God we didn't have any animals except outdoor cats. We had a beagle when I was about ten, and I would pet him but wash my hands right away. The same with the cats. I love animals, but I just can't be around them."

"But you did fine with step eight. You petted the rabbit and fed the ducks."

"Remember I can adapt to temporary situations. I already feel contaminated being here in the hospital, so it really isn't difficult for me to do activities I would normally avoid. I feel so dirty right now that nothing much would bother me."

"Do you think the behavior modification will change anything once you get home? Will it have any long term effects with your habits?"

"No, when I get home I'll clean up, and then I'll probably go back to my old ways. At least I've calmed down, and this really has helped me to relax. I'll probably never be as anxious as I was before I came to the hospital. I may have to come back here some day, maybe in another five or ten years if I feel I'm having a hard time functioning in daily life."

"When you get home, continue seeing your psychiatrist. Good luck with your progress and stay focused on what you've tried to accomplish," Dr. Montgomery told me as he was writing my discharge papers.

When I left the hospital, I drove 80 miles to my home. I felt that the inside of my car was contaminated as well as the door handle. I sprayed the interior of the car with Lysol until I could hardly breathe. If I had brought a suitcase instead of a paper bag to put my clothes in, I would have thrown the suitcase away. All of the clothes I had taken with me went into the laundry basket, and I took a 75-minute shower. I wouldn't sit on anything until I was clean again.

Those two weeks in the hospital seemed hardly to have helped me in coping in the real world. Just as I had told Dr. Montgomery, I went back to my old ways once I was home. For instance, I still couldn't keep items I felt were contaminated. Over the years, I had thrown out so many treasures. I was angry with myself for doing that, but my anger couldn't stop me from getting rid of them. Even when my diploma arrived at my front door in a manila envelope, I threw it away because it had been on the sidewalk. It was a beautiful diploma with my name engraved on it announcing my Master's Degree. But I couldn't keep it; it was dirty. Gifts put under the Christmas tree presented similar problems. I didn't throw them away, but I would tear the gift wrap off so the outside of the gift wrap did not touch the gift inside.

My summer of 1980, my time in the psychiatric ward, was over. I would begin teaching again in about a week.

CHAPTER NINE

I was really nervous starting my fourth year of teaching. I knew that Harry would still be monitoring my classes. The two weeks in the hospital really had helped. I was able to function normally again in the classroom. At least I felt I was as normal as I could ever be. I had worked hard to get my BA and MA degrees, and I wasn't going to give up without trying to change.

After a month, Harry quit observing me so closely. I was surprised to find out years later he had called my dad to talk about my problem. He knew my parents as he had been my brother's junior high physical education teacher. Harry told my dad I was staying seated at my desk and would not walk around the room to help students. I would help them if they came to my desk, but I seemed to be unable to be among the students. Harry informed Dad that I was becoming so incapable he was considering firing me. Dad told him he knew about my illness, and since he didn't have any answers, Harry should do whatever he had to do.

Leslie told me about Harry and Dad's conversation after my dad had died in 1991. Leslie had been living at home near the end, and my dad had confided in her before he died of cancer. He had never mentioned to me that I was so close to losing my teaching career. Dad didn't know how to deal with my OCD except to tell me not to wash my hands all the time. I think he felt sorry for Al, Leslie, and me because he realized our problems were caused by Mom. I could tell he was hurt and didn't understand what I was doing to myself. But he knew I was getting help, and all he could do was be supportive. If he had started yelling at me or forcing me to sit without being able to wash my hands, I would have freaked. I would not have gone home anymore, and I know he didn't want me to avoid coming home to visit. I was very emotional and needed the support of my family as there was no special person in my life to help me with my problem. If my principal had fired me, I think I would have committed suicide as teaching was my life.

When I returned to Wenatchee, I didn't see a psychiatrist. I was tired of talking about OCD to medical personnel. I just wanted to get away from it all, and somehow I managed to function quite normally for a while. But that didn't last. After almost a year, in June of 1981, I went back to Dr. Stevens. I was not doing well. I would go into his office, hyperventilating, and his secretary would hand me a paper bag to breathe into until I could get myself under control. I was worried the stress I was feeling was going to give me a heart attack. I had two EKG's within six months; my heart was normal. I was told to practice my tension reducing techniques, but I wasn't diligent with my efforts.

Besides my emotional problems, my body was behaving abnormally. I never had regular periods as I would have a menstrual flow about once every three months. I didn't get severe cramps, but I hated my periods because they were messy, and I felt unclean. I dealt with them from the time I was fifteen until I was 29. Dealing with them meant making myself clean. And I hated doing that. Despite my program in the hospital with shortened showers, I continued to decontaminate myself by taking excessively long showers.

I also felt the need to take a shower every time I had a bowel movement. Unless one has experienced the limitations from this particular obsession with staying clean, one cannot realize the full implications of what this entails. Imagine keeping track of all the food one eats, not because of bulimia or anorexia, but because one wants to have as few bowel movements as possible. I had learned how much I could eat so I could take a shower only every other day. This was better than every day as my showers lasted anywhere from 50 to 75 minutes. Sometimes I would pass out during or right after showering because I was so weak. When my body wasn't cooperating with me and I had to go to the bathroom more often, I would have to take additional showers to stay clean. I have a strict ritual that takes me through several steps before I feel clean again. My showers take even longer because I clean the shower faucet and sides of the shower stall.

I have been thankful for a long time I don't have to worry about cleaning the inside of my body as well. It would probably take me five hours to shower if I could take out my internal organs and separately wash them. Thank God we don't have to wash our heart, liver, kidneys, lungs, and other body parts separately. I know this is weird; I call it being crazy. I don't know why all the psychologists and psychiatrists I have seen over the years keep telling me that I am normal. Normal? I don't think so, but they keep reassuring me that there is no such thing as normal, and I only have a disorder.

By the time the last day of school arrived before Thanksgiving break, I was so weak I fell down. Because I had fallen on the rug, I needed to take another shower. I took a quick one that lasted only ten minutes as I was shaking and I could hardly stand up. I was not as clean as I wanted to be, but in my condition it would have to be all right. I got out of the shower and managed to dress myself. Somehow I drove the mile to my sister's place and walked up the stairs to her second-floor apartment.

"Leslie, let me in," I yelled as I swayed outside her door. When she opened the door, I immediately went in and collapsed on the couch. I was gasping for air, and the room was spinning around me.

"What's the matter with you?"

"Nothing, I'm just weak from not eating right."

"Marie, I think I should take you to the emergency room; you're as white as a ghost!" exclaimed Leslie.

"No, I just need to rest for a while. I'm too weak to drive home to Mom and Dad's house. Please call Al and tell him to come and get me." Al was home, visiting our parents for the holidays. Leslie was angry with me for insisting that I didn't need to go to the hospital. Al drove to Wenatchee and then drove me back home to our parents' house in Quincy. I kept my eyes closed. Mom and Dad were alarmed at my appearance, but I assured them all I needed was to rest and get some good food over the long holiday weekend.

I was in the middle of my period, but because I wasn't eating right, my period was not ending after a regular cycle. I had been bleeding for two weeks, and even though I tried to start eating right when I got home, I was unable to regain my strength. Losing blood made me weaker. I stayed in bed and ate as much as I could. By Friday night, Mom said she was going to take me to the clinic the next morning. She noticed that my fingernails had no color. Being a nurse, she knew that is one of the first signs that a person is very sick. I got up to take a shower the next morning and almost fainted from being so weak. Mom didn't want me to take a shower, but I insisted as I felt unclean. Mom took me to the clinic in Wenatchee. During the 30-mile drive, I kept drifting in and out of consciousness; I had trouble focusing and staying awake.

At the clinic, the nurse took one look at me and helped me to an examining room. She got the doctor who told her to take my pulse and blood pressure. They couldn't get a pulse let alone my blood pressure reading.

"Take her to the hospital emergency room and have the gynecologist on duty standing by," said the doctor.

Mom drove me to the emergency room, and I stumbled into the hospital. The nurse on duty was trying to get me to sit down in a wheel chair, standard procedure to enter the ER. I drifted by her mumbling I needed help. I was admitted for anemia and blood transfusion due to uterine bleeding. Dr. Halgren, the gynecologist on duty, was in surgery, but he immediately ordered three pints of blood for me. The body has eight pints of blood and I needed five, but as Dr. Halgren told me later, "It's better to give less blood and to let the body build itself back up naturally." I was lucky the blood wasn't infected with HIV as the national testing procedure for AIDS did not start until years later.

My body absorbed the blood. But my heart was pounding so hard that I thought it was going to burst. After I revived from the blood transfusion, I noticed Mom standing next to the bed. She was upset and couldn't understand how I would allow this to happen to myself.

"Marie, what are you doing? Are you trying to kill yourself? We all love you and want you to take care of yourself."

Killing myself seemed like a good idea to me.

Mom stayed with me until she had to drive home. I was in the hospital for a week trying to regain my strength. I told Dr. Halgren about my OCD and how I hadn't been eating because I didn't want to take more showers than I already did. I told him I was sick of having periods, and I wanted a hysterectomy because I couldn't deal with the uncleanness of periods.

"But you're only 28. Don't you want to have children someday?"

Bitterly I replied, "No, I don't want to have any kids as I would never put a child through what I had dealt with while growing up. I consider children dirty – they're in diapers, and they're always crawling on the floor. I don't want to touch anything that's unclean, even babies. I read an experiment in my psychology book about newborn monkeys who were denied physical contact with each other or humans. They all died. I'd never want to touch a baby, and I don't want to be responsible for the death of a child because I couldn't show any love. I wouldn't put a child through the hell I went through growing up."

"Are you seeing a psychiatrist?"

"Yes, I am seeing Dr. Stevens. He knows how I feel about having children, and I think he would agree with my decision."

"I'm going to ask him to have a conference with us," Dr. Halgren said.

When the three of us talked in my hospital room, the two doctors agreed that it would be best for me to have a hysterectomy. I told them I wanted to wait until next summer so I wouldn't miss any teaching time. Having a substitute teacher can lead to many problems for the returning teacher such as the students being undisciplined and falling behind in their studies. My first concern was my students, and I wanted to wait if the doctors agreed. I was scheduled for surgery in June 1982.

I also told them since I was Catholic, I wanted to check with the parish priest to see if a hysterectomy would be approved. The Church had changed since Vatican II in 1963. Rome still didn't approve of a young woman having surgery to avoid children, but Father King told me it was the best possible solution as I had nearly died. To someone who is not religious it may sound peculiar to want to receive permission from the Church for a surgery, but I am a cradle-to-grave Catholic. I didn't want to do anything against my church's teachings.

During the first few months of 1982, I continued seeing Dr. Stevens. He dispensed different samples of medication to me, but I didn't want to take most of them. Parnate gave me recurrent and persistent insomnia. Nardil caused me to move more, and I didn't like the dietary precautions I had to observe with other medications. If I was eating anything at all, I felt I was doing well. Being told I had to avoid certain foods did not help my state of mind or health. I was usually weak from eating correctly only every other day. I would eat a granola bar for breakfast and one for lunch. Then I would eat some cookies for dinner. The next day I would eat a hot meal at a restaurant.

I never bothered to cook at home as it was too much effort. I also had panic attacks if I had to go to the grocery store. There were too many people there with babies and little kids, and some of the people in the stores were not wearing clean clothes. I didn't want to get near any of them, so I avoided grocery shopping as much as possible. I had read in a magazine that a refrigerator needed to have several items in it for the appliance to work properly. I purposely kept four cans of soda in the refrigerator so the circulating air would have something to keep cold. Crazy? I think so, but I didn't want to have a repairman at my house. In fact, my OCD made me so dysfunctional that I wouldn't allow anyone, even family, in my place. I would always see Leslie at her apartment, and if Mom and Dad visited, we would meet at Leslie's place.

Dr. Stevens noted in my psychiatric file that "Miss Gius, on her own, discontinued the Nardil in spite of the fact that she was having a fairly good response to it and has once again restarted. Once again she had been eating erratically and in the strongest possible warning I suggest that she alter her diet to increase caloric intake. Current weight is 115, which is apparently the lowest she has been since high school. Also she is starting to have a bit of ringing in the ears, unrelated to the Nardil and was similar to some of the symptomatology that she had before. Also she has been prescribed Iron and B vitamins, which she has also been lax in taking. I have encouraged her strongly to follow the recommendation."

On June 21, 1982, I had a hysterectomy. I could no longer cope with the psychological effect menstrual bleeding caused me as my obsession with cleanliness and my abhorrence to periods was detrimental to my physical and mental health. My ovaries and tubes were not removed because their removal would have made me age prematurely. I was 29, and I took six weeks to heal. I was glad I had waited until the summer because I felt relaxed and was not worried about missing school. To this day I don't regret having had a hysterectomy. What I do regret is not having any children. I felt any child of mine would not be mentally normal. Living my own hell is enough. I was not going to put a human being through the experiences I had.

I had no desire to ruin another's life. I did not want a grown adult yelling at me that I had wrecked his or her life.

Every time I see a baby or small child, I get very emotional because I think about what my children would have looked like. I missed teaching them about life. I feel the main reason to live is to continue the human race. I denied myself this privilege. I know it is for the best, but I get depressed. I will be sitting in church crying silently because of what I have missed. It doesn't bother me much during the week when I don't see small children, but all I have to do is go to Mass, and I become emotional. I wonder why I even bother going to church. I know God knew exactly what was going to happen to me before I was born, and yet, He wanted me to be born. My mom was perfectly happy not to have any grandchildren. I think my dad would have loved to have been a grandparent. My sister had a hysterectomy in 1983, and my brother had a vasectomy before he married Darla, a registered nurse. The three of us didn't want to have children; we didn't want to teach them our dysfunctional habits and ruin more lives.

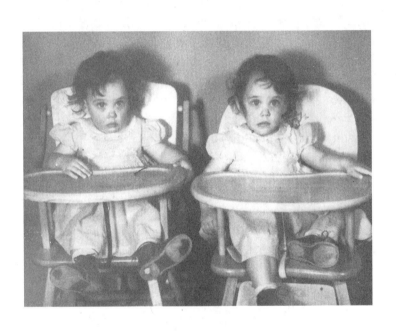

CHAPTER TEN

I told Dr. Jaecks, my internist, I was going to Washington, D.C. with a group of students from my junior high during spring vacation. I was nervous because I was not sleeping well, and Dr. Jaecks noted in my chart, "She is worried that something will happen to activate one of her compulsive behavior patterns and that she will be thought of as being weird. She does like to conceal these patterns generally."

The last statement about hiding my OCD is very accurate. I have learned many ways to cover up when something is bothering me. If I am walking down the street with someone, and I see something on the sidewalk that looks dirty, I will stop right where I am. I pretend I have something in my eye, and tell the person I am with to go ahead and I will catch up. I will walk out into the street to circumvent the dirty item. I'll do the same to avoid alleys, animals, people who do not look clean, and anything else that is bothering me. It is very dangerous as I have almost been hit by cars. While I am awake, I am constantly on edge. If someone approaches me, and I didn't know anyone was there, I will scream hideously. I not only scare the other person, but I also scare myself when I yell hysterically. I am very jumpy and nervous. If someone touches me on the shoulder when I did not expect it, sometimes I will turn around and swing at the person. It is an involuntary reflex due to my extreme nervousness.

Since I had finished my Master's Degree in 1980, I needed some activity to keep me occupied during the summer. I knew that if I didn't go to summer school I would be an emotional wreck by the time I started teaching again in the fall. Otherwise, I would stay inside my townhouse all summer and read books and watch TV to escape the world. My agoraphobia was affecting my health.

Teachers are required to take classes to continue their education after they have finished their Master's Degree or fifth year. I decided I would go to summer school and combine education with vacation. I attended the University of Hawaii during the summers of 1981 and 1983. (I had a hysterectomy in July of 1982.)

Since I had lived in Hawaii before, I should have known better than to spend several hours at the beach, even if it was an overcast day. I was crazy to stay so long, but I thought I might as well be at the beach for several hours because I would have to take an extra shower anyway when I returned to the dorm. I paid dearly for my mistake. I developed second degree burns that took two weeks to heal. My skin broke out in huge blisters, and it hurt to walk, lie down, and take a shower. The doctor at the student health center said, "You're lucky you have darker skin because if you were a blonde or a redhead, you'd probably develop melanoma."

I always enjoyed myself when I went away for the summers. But the fun never lasted. At the end of the season, I would return to my lonely apartment and become depressed. I had given up on the idea of ever being happily married; I resigned myself to living a lonely life and dying alone. I would get very angry with such thoughts, and I would remind myself that anger, like any other emotion, is something a person cannot control. What humans can control is how they react to anger or any other emotion.

I was so angry I wanted to walk into a fast-food restaurant and shoot people I didn't know. I felt that if I wasn't happy, why should others be happy? When one doesn't care about one's own life, it doesn't matter if one lives or dies. People who know me well would be shocked that I could think about destroying lives, innocent people as well as myself. The only idea I could continue to believe was God put me here for a purpose, and He loves me. I could not destroy anyone else just because I was hurt and angry about my life. It isn't right to take one's anger out on someone else. I felt guilty about even having an evil thought, but I couldn't help the way I felt. Again, one cannot help the emotions one experiences, but a person has a free will to act in a positive or negative way to the emotions.

I know my OCD has helped me have more empathy for others; for I know what it feels like to be enraged. I know how it feels to want to end life. I have always loved the Native American adage about not judging another until one has walked a mile in his footsteps. Does one person really know what another person is feeling or thinking? I understood why some of my students were so angry because they came from unacceptable living conditions involving sexual, verbal, or emotional abuse. My understanding helped me be more accepting of them and, I believe, a better teacher.

CHAPTER ELEVEN

In the summer of 1984, I attended Harvard. Dad was not happy I was going to Boston. He finally blurted, "Well, if you get raped, don't tell me about it!"

I assured him I would be careful. I left on June 18 with my sister and Mom. We flew to Philadelphia and rented a car. We drove through Connecticut, Rhode Island, Delaware, and New York. We arrived in Boston on Saturday, June 23.

I was able to adapt to the dorm because I had a room by myself with its own bathroom attached. In 1981 I had been in a dorm with a bathroom down the hall, and I had a hard time functioning. I still did not want to be in the bathroom if anyone else was present as I might get contaminated by a toilet flushing or someone washing her hands.

I enjoyed my eight weeks and took a writing workshop and a class on how to teach writing. The writing workshop was limited to 15 students, and we all would have a chance to present samples of our writing. Three people would present each time we met. Everyone would receive copies of the writings in advance so they could critique them. I decided to write about my OCD, but I used a different name and disguised everything so no one would know I was referring to myself. It was very therapeutic to put my thoughts on paper. I typed 32 pages before I was finished. At the time, my writing was stiff and formal. I wouldn't use one word by itself; I always had to have a complete sentence. Having a double major in English and Business Education reinforced the importance of correct usage of language. Later in life I became more open with my writing, and do not always use complete sentences.

I sent Dr. Stevens a letter from summer school to let him know how I was doing. I told him:

> *I love it here. I never knew people on the East coast could be so friendly. Everyone is so helpful including the policemen around campus.*
>
> *I am trying hard not to let objects or situations bother me. I found a Catholic church close to my dorm, so I plan to go to Mass every Sunday. This is good for me because it forces me to get out in the world. I have met students from all over the globe, and I enjoy hearing their opinions and learning about other cultures.*

I lived in a dorm by the Charles River, separating Boston from Cambridge. At the time Boston had over a million people, and Cambridge had 90,000. Growing up in the wide open West made it difficult for me to adapt to crowded conditions. I was glad summer school was only two months.

I had been on campus less than a week when I became ill with food poisoning. The only place I had eaten since I had arrived was the dining hall located in the dorm. I was admitted to Harvard's medical clinic, a five story hospital. I was on IV's and violently sick; other students became ill, but I was the only one hospitalized. I sent messages to my professors informing them I would miss class. My brother came to visit the night before I was discharged.

I was weak and told Al I couldn't walk far. We took a subway to the historical section of Boston and started walking the Freedom Trail. I had to stop and rest often. I told Al I couldn't go any further, so we returned to the dorm.

Since I was constantly worried about my life, I was receiving counseling from my family priest, Father Richard. He wrote me,

> I hope that you aren't worrying too much. The way I stop worrying is do my best and accept what comes and know that it all works out for the best in the end. Your thoughts on depression are very real and a lot of people experience it. It's hard to overcome sometimes. Depression can be tied into not finding the purpose and meaning to your life. We all need meaning and a purpose to survive. When we lose meaning, life becomes difficult. There is meaning and purpose to your life. You may not be married, but there are many other reasons to live. One of the significant things you do is help the students at school. You can't imagine how much you are needed when it comes to the impact of education. You are part of the web of life. We are all interconnected, and all are needed and useful. The difficulty is in recognizing how needed you are. I don't know if this makes any sense to you, but I see a lot of purpose in you. So keep going; you can conquer anything if you want to.

Father Richard was insightful and helped me tremendously. He is an excellent priest, but he would have been an excellent psychiatrist also. I knew I could continue existing if someone like him thought my life was worthwhile.

I continued teaching and attending summer school. I went to the University of Colorado in Boulder in 1985. The campus is nestled in a beautiful setting against the foothills of the Rockies. I enjoyed the two classes I was enrolled in, but the dorm was not acceptable to me because the bathroom had only toilets and sinks. I would have to go down the hall to a separate room to take a shower. When I feel contaminated from going the bathroom, I want to go immediately to a shower, not walk down the hall to another part of the dorm. I was able to switch dorms after two days. I was going crazy because of the situation. I remember going to the other dorm with a change of clothes and taking a shower there. I did this until I was able to get into a dorm that had all the bathroom facilities in one room.

I was very frustrated because I never dated and missed having a man hugging me. I was 25 in 1978 when I first had sex. I didn't feel anything at the time, and I was lucky I didn't get pregnant. I don't believe in abortion, but I often wondered what I would have done if I had become pregnant. If I had chosen to have the baby, I would have signed adoption papers. I would not have wanted to see the baby as that would have hurt too much. Fortunately, that was one situation I never had to confront.

Seven years later during the summer of 1985, I felt the need to go out with someone again. Although I must keep my home and myself meticulously clean, when I am away from home I am able to adapt well to different situations. I knew that being out of my usual environment while at summer school would present a better opportunity for me to date.

I was now 32, and I was still angry that I wasn't married. I wanted to have a husband. And I wanted at least two children. I knew I couldn't because of my hysterectomy, and I knew I shouldn't because of what any child of mine would be – someone like me leading a life of hell. I couldn't bring a new life into this world and do that to an innocent child. Yet still, I had a yearning for children and was mad with the life I had. I felt everything that was taken for granted by most humans was not allowed for me. I wanted to be married, but my OCD prevented me from even dating.

Every time I thought about my mental illness I became more angry. I missed physical companionship. I thought I might as well have a relationship. I'd have no fear of an unwanted pregnancy because of my hysterectomy. I started seeing a guy named Steve who was also attending summer school. We spent a weekend at his cabin, and I felt relief from being sexually active again. But being raised a strict Catholic and taught that sex outside of marriage was sinful, I was filled with remorse. My guilt was so great that I went to confession immediately. I still felt guilty even though God had forgiven me. We humans have a great propensity for refusing to forgive ourselves. I knew it would take years before I would quit feeling guilty.

I was glad to get back to campus because the cabin was not clean. I took a two-hour shower. I still felt contaminated, so I went to another bathroom in the dorm and took another shower. I was so exhausted I thought I was going to faint. Dating with intimate contact just wasn't worth the rituals I put myself through to stay clean. I didn't date again for six years. I continued to do activities with groups of people I met at summer school, but I wouldn't put myself in a situation where I'd be dating one person. Besides undergoing my exhausting cleaning ritual, I didn't want anyone to be around me long enough to realize I was different. I could cope more easily and feel safer in being a part of a group than in being with only one man.

Leslie and I moved into a townhouse in 1986. We had lived together a few times since high school, but each of us dealing with herself and the other, both with OCD in one house, was too much. We couldn't stay together in the same place for long periods of time. We were both depressed and fed each other's negative thoughts and feelings. We talked about committing suicide.

"Leslie, we were born together and since we're both so unhappy, we could die together by sitting in the car with the engine running in a closed garage."

Although we talked about it several times, neither one of us wanted to take the final step because we knew Dad would be crushed. Mom would also be devastated, but we didn't care. Suicide would have been easy. But Leslie and I didn't want to destroy Dad. After Dad died, we no longer wanted to commit suicide. Living wasn't any easier for us. Just the opposite: I believe it takes more courage to continue living. But we were not willing to take our own lives.

I continued teaching and attending summer school. In 1986 I went to the University of Minnesota in Duluth. Monte, a social studies teacher, had told me to go to Minneapolis as Duluth was too cold. I didn't take his advice. When I walked to my first class, I realized the campus was connected with tunnels. I like to be outside during the summer, so I pulled open a door and walked a fourth of a mile to another door. The door was locked, and I had to wait until someone came along in the tunnel and heard me pounding on the door. The grass was full of dew, and the fog was thick. I asked someone which way is Lake Superior as I couldn't even see it. I decided to take six credits in two weeks instead of the five week classes I was enrolled in at the time. Six credits in a short amount of time meant that I spent all day in class and the rest of the time doing papers and studying. I left Duluth and stopped in Pocatello, Idaho, to visit my brother for a week. I told Monte the first day of the new school year he was right about Duluth. It is a beautiful city, but I was not happy there.

In the summer of 1987, I went to the University of Hawaii again as Leslie was going to go with me. My brother had never been to Hawaii, so he came over and visited us for a week. Leslie and I lived in a student apartment. I was able to relax a bit because we had our own bathroom. We stayed for the six-week session and rented a car. I enjoyed going to the beach again, but my OCD bothered me. I would return from the beach and have to take another shower even though I had already taken a shower earlier in the day. Living in the apartment complex, we found it harder to meet people. Leslie and I didn't get involved in social activities. I enjoyed spending time with Leslie, but both of us having OCD just reinforced our habits.

The professor of my counseling class for teachers had a unique approach for us to learn more about the problems people dealt with by having us go to meetings for people with different disorders, such as alcohol abuse. I attended an Alcoholics Anonymous meeting and introduced myself as a friend of AA. One man told the group about being put in a Mexican jail and trying to overdose on strawberry soda and pills. He was not successful; he was taken to the infirmary and laid on a cement slab where he stayed until he regained consciousness.

I also went to an Overeaters Anonymous meeting. Another teacher in my class was also there, and we both sensed hostile feelings from the members in attendance. Out of the five women who were at the meeting, only one was 50 pounds overweight. The other women were only 20 pounds overweight, but they saw themselves as fat. None of them appreciated two slim people showing up, claiming to be friends, and expecting to listen in on their private revelations.

Still, they shared their experiences. One woman would eat everything in the cupboard. When there wasn't anything left to eat, she would tear up cereal boxes and chew on the cardboard because she had to have something in her mouth. Hearing others talk about their problems was therapeutic for me because it reminded me that I was not the only one suffering.

The last day of class the professor had us meet at the beach to watch the sun rise. I talked to him privately and explained why I wouldn't be there, but I did attend the breakfast at a restaurant after the class left the beach. I had missed another social event because of OCD. I hated myself.

In 1988 I was in a graduate dorm in Palo Alto, attending Stanford for summer classes. I quickly found out that the "graduate" dorms housed graduates from all levels, including students from high school, and not just those who had college degrees. There were two girls across the hall from me that had never been in a dorm before, and they were typical screaming freshman girls. I liked both of them, but they drove me nuts with their giggling and hysterics. Did I act like them when I first went to college? Yes, I thought, and now I knew what the junior student in our dorm meant when she talked about us freshman.

I was very nervous in the living arrangements as I didn't have my own bathroom. The dorm had been built for men; therefore, the showers had no dividers for privacy. Most women's dorms have separate shower stalls. I tried to take a shower when no one else would be using the bathroom, but I couldn't control whether anyone joined me. If I was almost done showering and someone came in and stood by me to start taking a shower, I would have to stay longer to feel clean. It was grade school all over again except this time I had to deal with people too near me in the shower, not just by the bathroom sinks. I went to see a psychologist on campus and had him write a letter that I needed to return home early because of my mental health problems. I had already finished my writing workshop, and I arranged with my other professor to do an extra project so I could leave early.

A teacher from Chicago named Ray was in my dorm. We didn't date during the summer, but we would go with others to activities on campus. He heard that I was leaving early and wanted to know what was wrong. I explained about OCD, and he felt sorry for me.

I was upset with my need to leave early, but I couldn't deal with the dorm anymore. When I returned to teaching junior high in the fall of 1988, I had my psychiatrist, Dr. Permut, write a letter that I could take with me to summer school. I missed my other psychiatrist, Dr. Stevens, who had moved to Virginia, but I knew Dr. Permut could also help me.

The letter was in memo form and said the following:

> *September 20, 1988*
> *RE: Marie H. Gius*
> *To Whom It May Concern:*
> *Because of a nervous condition, obsessive compulsive disorder, Marie Gius should be housed in an apartment or dormitory that has a private bathroom during her tenure with you. If she lives with others, her condition causes her to become so anxious that she becomes physically ill to the point where she cannot eat or function normally. She is under treatment for this disorder, yet the behavioral aspect requires her essentially to live by herself.*

During the summer of 1989, I attended the University of Florida at Gainesville. I took two weeks of classes with four hours of class time required every day. I again stayed in an apartment so I wouldn't have to use a public bathroom. I didn't want to be in any more dorms unless I could have my own bathroom. But I felt isolated and lonely being apart from others in the program.

To make matters worse, I knew my parents were not doing well. By this time my dad already had cancer, and

Mom was worn out from taking care of him. While Leslie stayed with Dad, Mom came to see me. After my classes were finished, we rented a car and drove to Disney World. We also went to the Florida Keys. I really appreciated my Mom spending time with me as she had already been to Florida. When Mom got on the plane to go home, I cried. I decided that since I had already finished my classes, I would also leave even though I was signed up for the apartment for another two weeks. Going home early gave me more time to visit Dad as he was not well.

Since I had been in the psychiatric ward in 1980, I continued seeing psychiatrists. In October 1989, Dr. Permut informed me Prozac was now approved by the FDA for patient use. He started me with a trial basis of 20 milligrams each morning. I again saw Dr. Permut in April 1990 and told him I had taken only 14 of the Prozac pills he had prescribed for me. He reiterated that I should give Prozac a chance because it might help me with my compulsions and obsessions. I started calling Dr. Permut instead of seeing him for therapy as the clinic was undergoing renovation, and I did not feel comfortable being in the building. I was able to cope in this way and keep teaching.

I was following Dr. Permut's advice about taking Prozac and found that it was helping me. He agreed. On June 5, 1990, when I saw Dr. Permut, he commented in my chart,

> *She has really responded nicely to Prozac. There is a bathroom for the staff in her school and for 11 years, she has been unable to use it due to fears of contamination. This will necessitate her walking down long hallways, out of her building, and into another building in order to find a bathroom to use. She would do this consistently, but since she has been on the Prozac she has been able to talk herself into using this other bathroom*

and has been successful in doing so. She is feeling more relaxed. She is allowing students to come up to her desk and approach her about certain matters and isn't feeling so guarded that they are somehow going to contaminate her. She feels this has made her a more effective teacher and actually has made teaching more enjoyable.

Dr. Permut was leaving the clinic and would be gone by the time I returned from summer school in 1990. He advised me to continue taking Prozac and eventually increase my dosage.

CHAPTER TWELVE

By the summer of 1990, I was tired of going to summer school, but I still had 14 credits left to reach 90 past my Master's Degree, which would put me at the top of the pay scale. Most teachers do this not only for the pay, but also because we are required to professionally maintain our competence level. I was debating on whether to attend the University of Wisconsin at Madison or Northwestern University in Evanston, Illinois. I always read university catalogs carefully to make sure that I will find courses interesting to me and housing that works for me. I was leaning towards Northwestern when I noticed in the UW catalog that an OCD group would be meeting once a month in the campus hospital. I was intrigued as I had always wanted to attend a group meeting, but there were no therapy groups in Wenatchee for OCD. The OCD group at Madison made my decision.

I was lucky that an old hotel on campus had been converted into a private graduate dorm which required students to be graduated from college, not just from high school. I had a huge room on the fourth floor with my own private bathroom. I took three classes during the eight

weeks. One was a health class required for all future teachers in the state of Wisconsin. Since AIDS had been around
for a while, everyone wanted to talk about Lyme disease,
which most of us didn't know about. Our professor was
excellent because we not only reviewed basic health issues,
but she also let us explore the most current concerns in the
world of health.

My other two classes dealt with the history of testing
in America and students' rights and responsibilities. I found
it interesting that the immigrants at Ellis Island were tested
before they were allowed into America. If they did not pass
the tests, they were sent back to their homeland. Imagine
some authority figure flashing cards. If a foreigner was tired
or sick, he probably wouldn't do well on the tests. The other
class explained how students gained power in the public
school systems. We studied court cases. The first involved
students wearing headbands to protest the Vietnam War.
The school district wouldn't allow the headbands, but the
Supreme Court upheld the students' right to wear them.

I studied for hours because I was taking 10 credits of
graduate level courses. Summer school is shorter than a
semester during the regular college year, so professors
expect more work completed in less time. I had been studying for two hours, and I needed a break. I went to the dorm's
TV lounge and started watching an old episode of *Family
Ties*. I had attended summer school every summer but one
since I had finished my Master's Degree in 1980, and I was
tired of forcing myself to get to know others and always
being the one to say hi first. So when I heard someone
enter the lounge, I didn't bother to turn around or say anything. I had also given up on dating, on marrying and having children, on finding someone special. When one lets
go, one usually then finds what one wanted all along. This

is what happened to me; I stopped looking and then found my special someone.

Doug Spaulding walked into my life. He saw me and said, "Hi, my name's Doug."

I thought how nice it was for someone else to break the ice. To this I could reply.

"Hi, my name's Marie."

"Where are you from?"

"Washington."

"DC?"

"No, Washington State. I wouldn't live in DC; it's too crowded. Where are you from?"

"Minnesota"

"Oh, really, which area?"

"Crystal, a suburb of Minneapolis. I have an aunt and uncle who live in Tacoma."

"I have a lot of relatives around the Tacoma area."

Doug had come to the TV lounge to take a study break. He was working on a Master's Degree in Library Science. I told him I was a teacher and taking credits to reach the top of the pay scale and for continuing education. We never went out during the eight weeks of summer school, but I kept seeing him in the TV lounge and where we picked up our mail. I had met a girl from Jamaica named Karen. We were going to go see *Born on the Fourth of July*, and I told Doug that if he wanted to join us he could. I was happy when he showed up for the movie. We talked and the three of us walked back to the dorm together.

"Marie, I'm taking you to Babcock Hall. We're in the dairy state, and some of the best ice cream I've tasted is here."

I was worried that Babcock was near a dairy farm, but Doug assured me it was in one of the buildings on campus.

He, of course, didn't know anything about my OCD. Once I felt okay about the location, I agreed to go for a milkshake.

I enjoyed walking to Babcock Hall. We talked more about our studies and our lives. Doug had an undergraduate degree from Augsburg, a private Lutheran University in Minneapolis. He had majored in history and philosophy and had minored in theology and political science. It was easy to talk to Doug as we shared the same interests. I never thought it would lead to anything. Halfway through the term, he went home for the weekend. I was sad because my brother who visited me from Idaho that weekend left before he and Doug could meet.

While I was attending summer school, I was able to go to two OCD meetings held in the psychiatry department of the campus hospital. About 25 showed up for the first meeting. We all looked at each other and wondered how the session would work. A nurse introduced herself as the facilitator of the group.

"My name is Sharon, and I am a registered nurse who has OCD. I had to quit working in my chosen field because I was checking each patient's chart 50 times to make sure I didn't give the wrong medicine. It got to the point where I couldn't do my job because I was spending too much time rechecking everything I had done.

OCD manifests itself in many ways. Most of my problems have to do with checking everything excessively. What I thought we could do is make a circle with our chairs and introduce ourselves to each other. Then different people could volunteer to tell their stories concerning their illness."

It is always awkward when a group of strangers gets together to discuss their problems. Now that we were all in a circle, we just looked at each other. I was trying to figure out who had the same symptoms as I had.

Since no one was talking, Sharon said, "I'll give some more examples of people dealing with OCD. One woman walks to the mailbox and counts every piece of mail. She backs up while returning to her house because she's afraid she's dropped something. She checks and walks backward up to 50 times. A man thinks he's hit someone when he's driving, so he drives around the block continuously, looking for a fallen pedestrian. He drives around the same block so many times someone calls the police thinking that he's casing the neighborhood for criminal intent. The stress becomes too much for him, so he no longer drives. Does anyone have a story to share with the group?"

One petite blonde introduced herself as Nancy. "I take a six-hour shower everyday."

Everyone was stunned by her remark, and for 30 seconds no one said anything. Finally someone asked, "Doesn't the water get cold?"

Nancy nodded her head yes.

"What do you do? You stand in cold water and time yourself for six hours before getting out of the shower?"

Nancy wrapped her arms around her body and nodded yes.

Again, we were shocked. I can't imagine staying in the shower for six hours. It's hard enough for me to take 40 to 60 minutes. Sometimes if I feel really dirty, I'll take longer. But six hours? I thought I was excessive. I know one can always find someone else who has worse problems. We all gave Nancy a sympathetic look, but there was nothing we could do to help her.

Marlene said, "I take forever to do the laundry because I clean off the inside and outside of the washing machine with Lysol."

I could relate to her as I also use Lysol to clean off the machine. If I accidentally touch a surface area that I already cleaned, I have to clean it again. It can take me 30 minutes to get one load of clothes in the washer.

"I do that also," I volunteered. "Even if I'm just washing my hands and I touch part of the sink, I have to start washing my hands over again."

"I check at least 50 times to make sure the stove is off," said Tom.

Our group leader replied, "This severely limits your ability to function in the house, doesn't it?"

"Yes, it does. I also have a problem with throwing anything away. I have boxes stacked to the ceiling with very narrow paths to get around the house. I think I have to save everything. It's stressful to have junk everywhere."

Sharon said, "This is a very common trait of OCD. Have you been seeing a doctor to get help?"

"Yes, but it doesn't seem to help me very much. I still save everything because I'm afraid I might need it later."

As more people shared their experiences, I was glad I was with a group that could understand me, but I also didn't want to hear what bothered others as whatever bothered them would start to bother me. I was going to be more crazy. Leslie told me she had never counted items until I mentioned to her it was a common practice performed by people with OCD. Just like living with Leslie, being around others was good for support, but the group also reinforced each other with more negative habits and ideas. I attended only one more meeting during the eight weeks of summer school.

I continued to see Doug in the TV lounge. I liked him, but I didn't want to know him better because of my OCD. Again, I kept my distance for fear of him or anyone else getting to know the real me. I believed that the real me didn't deserve to be loved by anyone because of my crazy habits. I knew my family loved me, but I never felt anyone else could love me.

The last night before I was to fly home, I wanted to say goodbye to Doug. I knocked on his door.

"Doug, my flight home leaves at nine tomorrow morning. I need to get some sleep, but before I go I want to let you know how much I enjoyed meeting you."

"Come on in; you have time to talk for a while."

I walked in and asked Doug, "When are you going back to Minneapolis?"

"I still have two days of final tests to take before I leave."

"My two graduate level classes didn't have finals; I did research and wrote papers all summer. I even had to do research in the law library. I was so intimidated to use the law library because I've never been in one before, but my professor told me the librarians would help me. He was right; they were very helpful."

"In library science classes we do research in every field. Madison is one of the top ten universities in the United States for its Master's program in Library Science. The university doesn't waste time with students who are looking for an easy ride."

"I was impressed with the two classes I took this summer from the same professor. He really pushed me beyond what I thought were my capabilities. Wisconsin and Minnesota have always been on the 'cutting edge' in education. I'm glad he insisted that I go to the law library when I didn't want to go."

"So, Marie, what are you going to do when you get back to Washington?"

"Spend some time with my parents. My dad is dying of cancer, and I'm trying to get as much time as I can with him. Then I start teaching again in three weeks. How about you?"

"I still have one more summer to complete my Master's. During the school year, I'll be substitute teaching and working at the public library."

We kept talking for three hours, but I knew our time together had to end.

"Doug," I said, "I've really got to get some sleep. I'm sorry I have to go, but I'm glad I had the chance to say goodbye."

"Marie, why don't we write to each other?"

"Write?"

I was so exhausted by the end of the teaching day that I didn't have the energy for much of anything. I might call someone, but my eyes hurt too much to write letters.

"Yeah, write to each other," Doug replied.

"Well, I'll tell you what I'll agree to do. If you write first, I promise to write back."

Doug accepted that, and we said goodbye to each other. The next morning I flew home. I never expected to see Doug again. What I didn't know at the time was Doug is a letter writer; six typed pages arrived at my townhouse the next week. I was amazed he had so much to say and wrote me so quickly. I sent him a return letter. We started corresponding on a weekly basis with our letters usually crossing in the mail.

During the spring of 1991, Doug sent me a letter saying he was thinking about flying to Washington to visit his aunt and uncle in Tacoma and wanted to know if he could visit me. I panicked. I was fine carrying on a long-distance letter-writing relationship, but I did not want anyone in my townhouse. I would teach all week, go out to happy hour with some of my friends on Friday, and then stay in my place until I had to face the world again on Monday morning. Twice a month, I'd spend the weekend at my parents, but I never had anyone come to my place. I wrote Doug and said I didn't want him to visit me. I figured he'd think that I didn't want to know him better, that I just wanted to exchange letters.

How do you explain to someone that you have OCD? I didn't want to write to him about my mental illness.

In July 1991, I saw Dr. Jaecks again. I was 38 and had stopped taking Prozac when school had ended in June. Why would I take medications and then stop taking them? I don't like to be dependent on pills. But Dr. Jaecks convinced me I should continue taking Prozac because I had shown improvement.

Meanwhile, Doug and I continued sending letters back and forth.

My dad's cancer was getting worse, so I decided against school that summer. Instead, I spent the time with Dad. I also went with Al to Australia for two weeks in late August. As usual, I didn't take a suitcase; I just took old clothes in a small handbag. I planned to leave everything behind except the clothes I was wearing when I left Australia. The flight reservationist was skeptical about letting me board the return flight to America because I didn't have any luggage.

I'm glad I had planned to leave everything behind because I had strep throat so everything of mine was contaminated. Since I got sick on a Saturday and clinics were closed, the tour guide took me to see a doctor at his home. He was working on his farm, and as he examined my throat, there were dogs and a goat nearby. I already felt so dirty from the trip that such a filthy environment didn't bother me. Normally I'd object to any animals being near me, but as I usually did on vacations, I adapted. I loved Australia, but I avoided sheep and farms.

CHAPTER THIRTEEN

I am glad I didn't go to summer school and I spent more time with my dad because he died after I started teaching in September. I was devastated; Mom had tried to prepare me for Dad not getting better, but I kept thinking he would be all right. I remember the phone ringing on a Saturday night, September 7, 1991. It was Mom telling me Dad had died an hour earlier.

I told Harry I planned to work during the week and drive to and from Quincy. Harry told me to take the five days allowed for a family funeral, that my mom, brother, and sister would need my support. I'm glad he insisted I take the time off. We had many people coming to the house to see us as Dad had been well-known in town.

I was trying to decide who I wanted to call about Dad's death. The first person I wanted to call was Doug. I realized I loved Doug. A calm feeling came over me, and all I could think of was letting Doug know my dad had died.

I called and his dad, Ron, answered. Evidently he thought I was Doug's cousin Maureen and told me he would let Doug know I had called.

When Doug came home from working at the library, his dad told him he'd gotten a call from his cousin Maureen. Doug called her, and she told him she hadn't called. Meanwhile, I begin to wonder if Doug had gotten my message. I called again, and this time I talked to Doug. Once we cleared up the miscommunication problem, he was very sympathetic, and I was glad I could talk to him about my dad dying.

The funeral for Dad was on September 12. I cried because I had lost the person I loved the most. It was difficult to start teaching again, and one day I started crying in class. A student complained to the counselor. I was told not to worry about it as he knew I was a good teacher. I thought it was callous of someone to complain, but human nature can be ugly.

I decided to write Doug a letter in October telling him I loved him. It's a big risk to open one's heart to someone else, but Dad had always taught me the worst anyone could say is no. I decided to take a chance and see what kind of response I would get. Twelve red roses arrived with a card attached saying, "thinking of you."

I was thrilled and surprised at Doug's reply. Even though I was numb because my dad had died, I felt there was someone special in my life. We continued corresponding and decided to meet in Tucson during Christmas break.

Two months later, we were sitting on the couch in our suite at the Radisson when I said to Doug, "I have something to tell you."

"What? You have a boyfriend?"

"Do you think I would come all this way to meet you if I had a boyfriend?"

"Well, I know some girls who would. I once dated a girl who I found out was engaged. She didn't wear her ring because she thought she might meet someone else that she liked better. I dumped her as soon as I found out. Another girl I was interested in finally told me that her 'partner' would not want her going on a date with me. I had no idea she was a lesbian."

"No, Doug, that's not what I'm like. I do believe in being completely honest, and I want you to know I can't have children. If you want to get serious with someone and have children someday, I'm not the one for you. I had a hysterectomy in 1982."

"I don't want any children. I've taken care of my two nieces who were born in 1984 and 1987. I enjoy taking care of them, but I don't want any children of my own."

It was a relief to me Doug didn't want children. I wanted to tell him about my OCD, but I decided to wait for two days as I did not want to feel as if I was being watched for peculiar behavior.

We talked, swam, visited his friends, and saw the tourist attractions. We went to old Tucson, which is set up as an old West town. Doug asked me if I wanted to take a stagecoach ride. He never realized being around horses bothered me. I was able to go to the old West theme town because I was on vacation, and I was more relaxed. However, I didn't want to get by the petting zoo or the horses. The third night I told him about my other secret.

"Doug, I have something else I need to discuss with you. I have OCD. It means obsessive compulsive disorder. I wash my hands continuously; I'm obsessive about cleanliness. Have you ever heard of OCD? It's a mental illness. I wanted to tell you about it the first night we arrived, but I was too nervous, and I didn't want to feel I was being watched every second."

"I've never heard of it. What do you mean you were afraid of being watched?"

"Usually when I tell someone about OCD, I notice the person observing me very closely to see if I will do anything abnormal like washing my hands excessively or avoiding something that makes me feel contaminated. It limits what I do, but it's not dangerous to others; it affects only me. Since I am taking medications, I was able to meet you here in Tucson for vacation. I wanted to see you during spring break last April when you suggested meeting during your visit to your aunt and uncle in Tacoma. Doug, I panicked because of my problems. I know you were hurt when I wrote that I didn't want to see you and wanted only to write to you. But I didn't want you coming to my townhouse."

"Yeah, I thought you wanted me just as a friend, not to pursue a relationship. What do you mean you didn't want me in your place?"

"My OCD makes me very nervous. I don't want anyone to visit me. Even when my identical twin was living in Wenatchee, I would go over to her place. She never came to visit me."

"So instead of my visiting you, we just kept writing, and you stayed home during the summer because your dad was so ill. He died in September. What made you decide to see me now?"

"Remember you were the first one I called about my dad dying. I realized I loved you, and I wrote you a letter telling you how I felt. I thought I'd take a chance. I took another chance in seeing you and telling you about my OCD."

"Are you saying that now you don't mind if I visit you in Wenatchee?"

"I think I'll be okay. Let's just see how this vacation works out. If you can deal with my OCD in a suite setting in a hotel, then I think you'll be able to visit me in Washington."

"It sounds like a good plan. We'll take it one step at a time. So tell me more about OCD."

"Well, I'm very nervous about becoming contaminated by an object or a person that doesn't look clean. I want to take an hour shower if I feel dirty. I avoid going places and doing a lot of activities because of my illness. I flew here to meet you because I wanted to see you even though I have difficulties dealing with everyday life."

"Marie, I don't know how this is going to work out, but as you said, let's just see what happens. I'll try not to make you nervous or self-conscious."

"Thanks, Doug, that's all I ask at this point."

"Now," said Doug, "I have something to show you. It's a medical record stating that I don't have AIDS. I went to the doctor and had a blood drawing, so you could see the results. I know I don't have any diseases, but I want to show this to you in case we decide to become intimate."

I was dumbfounded that Doug would be so considerate. The concern he had shown overwhelmed me and I told him that I appreciated the thought. It made our relationship more special. I had no qualms about being intimate with Doug.

We enjoyed being together in Tucson for Christmas break, and we decided we would keep writing. Doug planned to visit me the following April. Every week Doug and I would wait for letters from each other. His usually arrived on Thursday, and I couldn't wait to get home after school to check the mailbox. We also called each other. Time went by, and Doug flew to Seattle as planned. He came to see me in Wenatchee, but my mom wanted him to stay in a motel. She offered to pay for the room, so Doug and I didn't object. My teacher friends wanted to meet Doug, so I arranged a happy hour at Barney's, a local sports bar.

Mike, a good friend and social studies teacher, said, "You have a lot of friends on the staff, Marie. We're going to check this guy out and make sure he's okay."

Knowing the jokes the teachers were capable of pulling, I was leery of what Mike and the others had planned for Doug at happy hour. Ed came in with an envelope full of old keys and poured them out on the table.

"Well, Marie, since you have a boyfriend, I guess we don't need these keys anymore."

I just laughed as I had told Doug to expect anything. He enjoyed meeting all the teachers, and we had a great time.

One morning Doug said, "Why don't we have breakfast at your place?"

"I don't eat breakfast but come over anyway."

Doug came, but he didn't have much of a breakfast. "Marie, this cereal has a "sell date" from a year ago."

"I'm sorry, Doug, but I told you I don't eat breakfast. How about dinner here instead?"

"Sure. We can make spaghetti. Do you have a garlic press?"

"Um, no, I don't."

"Do you even know what a garlic press is?"

"I assume it's something that presses garlic."

"How about a cast iron frying pan?"

I shook my head no.

"A colander?"

"Yes!"

"Marie, do you even know what a colander is?"

"Hey, I'm not a dummy. I never cook, but I *do* know how. Mom taught me, but I just don't bother cooking."

Doug did come for dinner, but he made the meal. The next day we visited his Aunt Lila and Uncle Les in Tacoma. I took Doug to Bremerton on the ferry, showed him Mt. Rainier, and did other tourist activities. I had a hard time saying goodbye to him at the airport. Our parting was bittersweet, however. Soon enough we'd be saying hello again; we planned to see each other in the summer.

CHAPTER FOURTEEN

By June of 1992, I was fatigued and lacked energy most days. Although my OCD continued to be fairly stable, I still had many of my compulsive traits, such as the necessity to shower after each bowel movement. My long showers were exhausting, and I worked to minimize them. I kept track of every piece of food I ate to make sure I didn't eat too much and to minimize the frequency of my bowel movements. Regulating my food like this meant I wasn't getting proper nutrition. This whole process was extremely stressful, not just to my body but also to my mind. I would continuously replay what quantity of food I ate, and it made me nervous to monitor my food intake. It is very common for people with OCD to control their bodies because they feel they cannot control their minds. I had power because I could decide what I would and would not eat. I am glad I wasn't bulimic as the thought of throwing up on purpose disgusted me.

I had continual nightmares where I was running away from situations that horrified me. In my dreams I would be in a contaminated area such as a garbage dump, and my body would be jolted awake to escape. I was taking 40 milligrams of Prozac a day, but that didn't seem to be enough for me to feel comfortable in dealing with the world. But I didn't want to increase my dosage because I'm afraid to take too much medication. I tried to cope, but I wasn't doing very well. I was hyperventilating and needed to blow into a paper bag to calm down.

I was glad when summer vacation started. Mom and Dad had always wanted to go steam boating on the Mississippi River, but Dad died before they had a chance to go. Mom still wanted to take a trip, so we went from St. Louis to St. Paul in the summer of 1992. Doug picked us up the next morning at the St. Paul Hotel, and we took Mom to the airport. I stayed with Doug and his parents, Gail and Ron, for a week. His parents made me feel as if I had known them all my life.

Doug also introduced me to his brother, Dan, his wife, Gayle, and their children, Neissa and Nicole. We took Doug's nieces to the park to feed the ducks. Nicole, a very bright eight-year-old, was not easily fooled by Doug's sense of humor involving outlandish feats performed by eating sauerkraut. Doug is seven-eighths German and loves to tell stories about strong Germans. Neissa, four years old, was a young lady in a child's body as she didn't scream or run around.

In the fall of 1992, I started teaching again for the new school year. My OCD still bothered me, but I was able to cope. I had not seen a psychiatrist since Dr. Permut had left Wenatchee in 1990. Dr. Jaecks, my internist, had continued the dosage of Prozac that Dr. Permut had prescribed. On December 14, 1992, my depression was worse. I didn't feel life was worth living. I told Dr. Jaecks I wished I was buried next to my dad.

During Christmas break, I visited Doug in Minnesota. I was glad I had someone special in my life to share the holidays with. My brother had gone home to Mom's place for Christmas. It was strange for me to not be with my family, but I felt I was adopting another family as Doug made me happy and comfortable. It helped my depression to have Doug interested in me.

I met Doug again in Tucson during spring break of 1993. We were at Pizza Hut, and the subject of marriage came up. We decided to become engaged and get married in August before I started teaching again and after Doug had finished his Master's. We went to a mall, and I found a ring. Doug and I were happy; I couldn't wait to return to teaching after spring break to show my friends my ring. When school started a week later, most of the staff and students didn't realize I had an engagement ring. Word leaked out slowly, and I was congratulated. I was 40 years old and had never been married. Doug got the same reaction from family and friends in Minnesota except they were asking him if this was my second or third marriage. They were surprised that I had never been married.

In addition to the excitement in having my first wedding was the thrill in realizing my secret wish was coming true. As much as I had dreamed of getting married, I had never really thought I would. After having given up all hope, I could hardly believe I had found someone I loved and who loved me and wanted to spend the rest of his life with me. So all the activities associated with my getting married gave me tremendous pleasure. I especially appreciated the wedding shower given by my friends. My mom's friends in Quincy also gave me a shower. They didn't know what I needed and said to Mom that I wouldn't need any kitchen supplies because I already had them.

Laughing, Mom replied, "Believe me, Marie has very few kitchen items. She doesn't cook so she needs just about everything."

The rest of the school year went by rapidly. Harry was leaving for a superintendent's position, so we had a going-away party for him at a restaurant. Paula told me that she and Candy had a gift for me as well. But I panicked when I saw it was in a bag on the floor. I told her I'd take the present, not the bag. When she handed me the bag, I made sure I touched only the handles. I planned to take out what they had given me and return the bag to Paula. My face turned beet red when I pulled out a teddy, and I quickly shoved it back in the bag.

Paula asked with a twinkle in her eye, "Are you sure you don't want the bag?"

I decided to keep the bag after all.

Doug was finishing up his Master's at Madison, so I told him I would take care of all the wedding details. We were going to be married in Wenatchee. I didn't want to spend a lot of money on decorations, flowers, or expensive backgrounds. My wedding dress was a simple yet beautiful gown that cost $140. I had pretty flowers ordered, but I didn't have any excess. I was pleased when people told me they enjoyed the ceremony because it wasn't showy. I wanted Leslie to be my maid of honor, but her back was bothering her. She couldn't stand for the length of the ceremony. Instead I asked my best friend and old college roommate to by my matron of honor. Lorraine, her husband Steve, and their two children Jessica and Rachel, came over from the Seattle area for the wedding.

Doug asked his brother, Dan, to be his best man. Dan commented, "I feel like one of those Chippendale men in this tuxedo."

Nicole, his nine-year-old daughter declared, "I know who Chip and Dale are."

"Oh, no, Nicole, your dad's talking about a different kind of Chippendale," I commented with humor in my voice and with no intent to explain the difference.

The innocence of children fascinates me. I started thinking about the children I would never have and what I was missing in life. Even though I thought I had forgiven my mom a long time ago, my resentment towards her flared up constantly.

Doug's nieces, Neissa and Nicole, walked down the aisle together carrying a four-foot long arrangement of flowers. I married Doug Spaulding, but I kept my maiden name because I did not want to change legal documents, including my driver's license. It would be too tedious and time-consuming.

We had a reception with dinner and dancing. Getting married at 40 is different from weddings for couples in their 20's. By 10 p.m. there were only two couples left besides us. We told the band they could quit early. We had so much wine left over we hosted a happy hour at our townhouse at the end of the first week of school. For me to be able to have a party where I lived was a major step. Being on Prozac, still 40 milligrams a day, had calmed me. I considered the drug to have worked a miracle: I was married where I never thought I'd be able to live with anyone.

Adjusting to married life was easy for me as Doug was understanding and patient with my habits. He started subbing while I continued teaching, but the work for subbing was sporadic. Doug had applied for a library position at a local elementary school, but someone who did not have a Master in Library Science (MLS) got the job. In Minnesota, an MLS is required to work in the school libraries but not so in Washington. He became so frustrated from not working he decided he would drive back to Minnesota to get a job. I didn't want him to go, but he was used to working

16-hour days between subbing and being in the library, and he found it intolerable to sit all day at home.

The morning he left I was so sad. I knew if he found work I would follow him because I did not want to be separated. He stopped in Quincy and visited my dad's grave. He continued east on Interstate 90, but while he was driving, he decided it wasn't right to leave me.

I had been feeling depressed all day when Monte told me there was someone in my room waiting to see me. I thought it was a student needing help with an assignment. I started down the stairs, and Doug started up the stairs. He had a rose and told me he just couldn't leave. I started crying. We hugged, and I told him I was so very glad he was back.

At Christmas we visited his family in Minnesota. One night Doug thought he was being funny when he wore an Arabian turban to bed. I had crawled in bed with the light off, so when he flipped on the light I screamed. For an instant, I wondered where Doug was, and who in the world was this man. Doug started laughing. He told me he had tried to sell me to Abdul, the camel driver, but since I wouldn't clean out the camel's stall, Abdul had reneged on the agreement. I thought I was worth at least two camels, but Doug said that he could get Abdul to trade him only a goat for me.

As the year 1994 started, I developed pneumonia. I spent a week in the hospital, and Doug was vigilant that I got the best care. I finally had finished the 90 credits required for the maximum amount allowed on the pay scale by taking classes locally. Except for two summers off, I had been in summer school since 1978. I was relieved not to have to go anywhere or study for more credits.

Since I had married Doug, I was eating more, including breakfast. Eating more meant I had to take more showers, but I felt better eating properly. I would bring deli sandwiches for lunch, and the teachers told me Doug should open a restaurant. After six months of marriage, Doug noticed I had gained five pounds. "Do you realize if you gain ten pounds per year, in five years you'll weigh 190 pounds?"

I had always wondered how people became so overweight. It was an epiphany to realize that it happens gradually without a person being aware. I started watching my caloric intake; I had never taken a diet pill, and I wasn't going to start now. My weight had been erratic for years due to my OCD, but I had never weighed 145 pounds. At only 5' 4", I have to be careful not to pack on the pounds.

Doug was called to substitute teach more after we found out the district office had only listed him as a substitute librarian. Being a substitute is not easy as students challenge the sub's authority. Doug was strict and would not let the students slack. Word gets around fast in a school district whether someone is a good sub or not. And the word about Doug was good: he was responsible and taught the students instead of baby-sitting them.

CHAPTER FIFTEEN

As the year 1995 approached, I was on Lorazepam and Prozac. My medication for Lorazepam was adjusted because the original dosage made me too sedated. With the change, I was tired at the end of the day, but I was more settled. I was able to maintain my equilibrium until the fall of 1995. I was stressed and nervous when I went to see my internist, Dr. Jaecks. I was talking very rapidly and was anxious. I was not doing well. My OCD had come back in full force, and I wasn't coping in the classroom.

Some of my students were aware that I had an aversion to the waste basket, and I would keep it in the far corner of the room under the pencil sharpener. Sometimes a student would move the waste basket right next to my desk while I was on hall duty between classes. I would act as if the waste basket didn't bother me when I entered the room again and saw it by my desk, but it did bother me. The students noticed it. I stopped going into the hallway between classes, so I could watch my room. If I saw a student moving the waste basket, I would tell him to put it back as the janitor wanted it right under the pencil sharpener to catch pencil shavings.

Doug was getting impatient with substituting, and I couldn't blame him as he was qualified in so many subjects. The East Wenatchee School District had few positions available each year, especially in history and library science. Unfortunately for Doug, Washington State does not require a person to have an MLS to be a school librarian. In Washington, a teacher who is tired of the classroom can easily become the librarian. This is not the case in Minnesota – an MLS degree is required – so Doug applied for a job in Minnesota. There was always the possibility that he would be hired; I would move back with him, but the uncertainty of our situation and the possibility of my having to adapt to a new environment added to my stress.

While taking a one-credit computer class at the high school on Saturday, I went to a bathroom in a different section of the building so I wouldn't have to be near anyone. The bathroom was unoccupied but as soon as the door shut behind me, I could not find the light switch. I panicked as I was by now several feet into the bathroom, and I was terrified of running into a waste basket. I stood there and started to cry and yell. No one heard me as I was too far from the computer room. I screamed for five minutes.

Finally, I realized that I would have to feel my way along the wall and pray that I didn't run into a garbage can or waste basket as all of them were contaminated. I took baby steps and tried to force myself to remain calm by breathing deeply. My heart was palpitating rapidly, and by the time I found the door, I was sweating and shaking. I went into the hallway and thanked God I had not touched a waste basket as it would have required me to take another long shower. If my clothes had become contaminated, I would not want to drive home in my car as I would get the car seat dirty. One of the most annoying traits of my OCD was how I related significant parts of my obsessions to other connected events. So I was especially upset about touching trash cans, but I felt the same way about anything that touched them. It was similar to my experience in high school with the dissected cats. I didn't want to touch someone who had been touching the dead animals. I couldn't stay for the rest of the class as I had to go home and lie down.

As I was telling Dr. Jaecks my problems, I was jumping around from one subject to the next with pressured speech and extreme nervousness. I told Dr. Jaecks that I was exhausted at the end of the school day and falling behind in grading papers. I felt I probably needed to see a psychiatrist again. He agreed and informed me that if I was not better in two weeks, I needed to schedule an appointment for a psychiatric referral.

I started seeing Dr. Donna Shaw in November 1995. I was 42 and taking only 20 milligrams of Prozac at the time. My medication level would vary according to my level of depression. If I felt I was doing well, I would take fewer pills. I was sporadic with caring for myself by taking the prescribed dosage of drugs. I found when I decreased my level of medication my depression increased. This was obvious to me, yet I still thought I had control of my mood swings. Dr. Shaw instructed me to take 40 milligrams a day of Prozac in the morning and another 20 milligrams in the afternoon.

I told her about my background. "My major concern, Dr. Shaw, is germs and contamination. My husband does all the cleaning as I will clean until I faint. I had a hysterectomy in 1982 because I couldn't tolerate the feeling of being gross and dirty during my period. I also wanted to be certain I'd never have children and raise them the way I was raised. I resent not having children, even though it was my own choice. I have been cheated out of one of the most important events in my life because I will never be a mother."

Dr. Shaw stared at me, and she then continued writing notes.

"I love animals, and I want to have an indoor cat. Every time I drive home I see a cat sitting on the back of a sofa looking out the picture window of one house on my street. I become depressed when I think about not having a cat. I can't have a pet because animals are dirty, and I can't stand being near them. I can't tolerate anything that I think is unclean. I wanted to start seeing you a few months ago, but I don't like this old, dirty house your office is located in."

"Oh, dear, my husband and I have a dog. She's a hunting dog who was traumatized because someone stole her. We just got her back, and she cries if she's left alone all day. Are you going to be able to cope with her being in the house?"

"Yes, as long as I never see the dog. Please don't bring her in this room either."

"Oh, no, she is afraid of strangers and stays in the back bedroom. How were you able to convince yourself to come to this house where my office is if you think it's an old, dirty house?"

"I was desperate enough to seek help again; I managed to convince myself I could walk in here as long as I stayed in the front part of the house. I didn't want to walk around the back where the alley is. To me, alleys are especially dirty, so I was okay avoiding that part of your house."

"How do you cope with grocery or clothes shopping?"

"My husband does the grocery shopping as I have panic attacks when I enter the store because there are people walking around wearing dirty clothes from working in construction or in the orchards. Before I was married, I usually didn't prepare food at home so I rarely went to the grocery store. Instead, I would usually eat in restaurants. But I also have found that my OCD bothers me more the older I get. Doug, thank God, is understanding about my illness and doesn't mind shopping. I don't go to clothing stores very often, especially malls because I don't want to be in crowds. I usually shop in the first part of January when the stores are empty. Super Bowl Sunday is a great day to go shopping as the malls are deserted."

"Marie, I want to monitor your progress with the additional milligrams of Prozac. You've never taken 60 milligrams a day; I need to see you on a continual basis to make sure this higher dosage works for you."

I continued seeing Dr. Shaw, but I was getting worse. "Doug, I think I'm going to have to resign from teaching. I can barely make it through the day, and I think I'm getting an ulcer. Would you mind if I quit at the end of the school year? I'm beginning to think moving back to Minnesota is a good idea; the chance of your getting a permanent position here is next to zero. The public library has only seven full-time positions, and the schools keep replacing retired librarians with burned out teachers. I know some of the teachers take additional credits in library science, but some of them don't."

Doug was uncertain what to do as he did not want me to give up my career when I had worked so long and hard to achieve the goals I had accomplished. We decided to wait and see how I was doing in two months. We went to Minnesota to visit Doug's family for Christmas. On a Friday afternoon in late February 1996, Doug and I were sitting at the local sports bar, waiting for other teachers to arrive for happy hour. I was sitting resting my head on the table as I was so tired I couldn't keep my eyes open.

Doug looked at me and said, "You know, maybe moving to Minnesota isn't such a bad idea."

I was speechless. "You mean it, Doug? You wouldn't mind moving."

"No, I've been watching your health deteriorate; you can hardly function. If you really think it would be best for you to quit teaching, I won't try and talk you into staying."

"I'm having trouble making it through the day. I'm so nervous and panicked around the students. My stomach hurts, and I am burping a lot. I don't feel as if I can physically or mentally maintain my health. At the end of the day, all I want to do is come home and flop on the sofa."

On March 20, I saw Dr. Jaecks for a consultation. I was 43 and burned out from teaching. I had continued seeing Dr. Shaw, who had increased my Prozac to 80 milligrams a day. The amount of Prozac helped, but my symptomatology had increased. My compulsion level was high; I was stressed and anxious.

"I don't think I'm going to continue teaching after this year, Dr. Jaecks, because of my physical and mental health. I'm beginning to wonder if I'm going to make it to the end of this school term. I don't want to quit early and leave the students in an upheaval. It's hard enough for junior high students to deal with school, but having their teacher quit in the spring of the school year is even harder for them. I know they have five other teachers for class each day, but the students resent subs."

"I recommend that decisions involving major changes be postponed until you're feeling better. Maybe you should wait until the summer break to decide whether to resign from your teaching position. A leave of absence is another alternative to consider."

I told him I'd discuss it with Dr. Shaw when I'd see her on April 9. By the time I saw Dr. Shaw, I had made my decision. I went to see La Verne at the superintendent's office. She was the bookkeeper responsible for keeping records of teachers' sick leave. La Verne told me I had accumulated enough sick leave in 19 years of teaching to

quit immediately; I wouldn't have to wait until the end of
the school year in June. Still, I didn't want to leave the students suddenly, so I decided to finish the school year.

"I can't guarantee I'll be at school five days a week. I'll
probably have to stay home at least one day a week and
maybe twice a week sometimes. Would the district let me
continue teaching as long as possible? I'm incapable of
working a full week anymore because I'm so nervous and
have such difficulty functioning in class."

"Yes, Marie, but it's your health that you should be most
concerned about, not whether you can make it until June."

I let my principal know what was going on. When I
explained my decision to Mr. Spurgeon, he was relieved
I was going to stay for the rest of the school year. He told me
to take as many days as I needed, but he appreciated the fact
I was not leaving the students during the last two months of
school. Mr. Spurgeon was supportive of my decision, but I
really missed being able to talk with my former principal,
Harry, with whom I'd had a good rapport.

It was such a relief finally to have made a decision.
Even though I was absent at least once a week, I was able
to finish the school year. Doug subbed for me, and since he
knew exactly what the students were doing and what I
expected from them, it was not a hardship for them to continue with their studies. One day Doug asked a kid who
was being obnoxious if he would be acting this way if I
were there. He shook his head no, and Doug told him he'd
better wise up or he'd be in trouble with me. I was a strict
disciplinarian who expected my students to behave and to
work to the best of their ability. Many students didn't like
me because they thought I demanded too much, but the
students who were serious about their education appreciated my efforts. I once had a student who was now a junior
in high school tell me that he had worked harder and learned

more in my ninth grade class than he had in any English class at the high school. I always felt good when I heard positive comments from parents, students, and former students that appreciated my efforts.

The school year finally ended on June 7. I went in for my annual medical checkup and told Dr. Jaecks I was still having an upset stomach. I asked him if he thought I should have an upper GI (gastrointestinal) surgery, but he didn't think it was necessary. I was bubbling over with enthusiasm as a lot of pressure and stress was gone. I had seen the same effect take place with many other teachers over the years who had decided to quit or retire. I, however, was not retiring, but I knew I didn't have a choice about staying in the classroom as my OCD prevented me from living a normal life.

CHAPTER SIXTEEN

Doug and I moved to Minnesota in August 1996, traveling across country with one car and a U-Haul. Doug's dad helped us by driving the U-Haul. I would take turns driving the car with Doug. I could drive for two hours, and then I would have to let Doug drive. All the medications I was taking made it difficult for me to stay fully alert for any length of time. I had been switched to Luvox for a while, but I went back to Prozac as the former gave me insomnia. We arrived at Doug's parents' house on August 13. It took us a week to get settled in at our house, and Doug applied for work with the Minneapolis library system. He started working as a substitute in several libraries.

On August 28, Doug's 63-year-old aunt died of cancer. I really liked Enid, and I took her death very hard. The next day Doug's mom and I went to Pet Smart, and I decided I could no longer live without a cat. Life was too short; I didn't want to die without ever having an indoor cat.

Pet Smart had a program established with the local humane societies to make it easier for people to adopt cats and dogs. The Plymouth store had nine cats ready for adoption, and I chose one that reminded me of the first cat we

had when I was nine. The name on the cage said "Tigger."
I disliked the name and immediately renamed her Sammy.
She was a beautiful three-year-old tabby who had to be given
up by her owners because they lived in an apartment. I told
Gail that I wanted this cat, and in my mind, she already
belonged to me. We walked to a restaurant, and I called
Doug on his mom's cell phone. He wasn't there. I panicked; I tried calling him again and again. I told Gail I knew
I should talk with Doug first before getting a cat, but when
she saw how upset I was, she told me to go ahead and adopt
Samantha. The nine cats had already been at Pet Smart for a
week, and I was convinced someone else would adopt "my"
cat. Gail and I let the store clerk know which cat I had chosen. He handed Samantha, Sammy for short, to Gail. The
cat was scared, and it required all of Gail's strength to hold
her. We bought her a litter box, a food tray, and cat food.

There was a five-year-old boy standing beside me. He
looked at me and said, "Are you going to get that cat?" I
nodded yes, and he said, "I've been coming here all week
to look at the cats, and this cat is the best one."

I looked at Gail and we smiled at each other. A truer
testimony could not be found anywhere as no one had paid
the little boy. We walked up to the vet department at the
front of the store, and I knew what a woman felt like just
after giving birth. I was so proud of my cat, and I told the
clerk that her name was Samantha. The vet was glad to see
someone adopting an adult cat as most people wanted kittens. Every animal needs a loving home, not just kittens
and puppies. Sammy crawled around on the bookshelves
in the doctor's examining room. The vet gave her a feline
leukemia shot, and she was ready to go to her new home.

I drove while Gail held onto the carrying box the clerk
had put Sammy in for the trip home. She was thrashing,
and it was hard for Gail to keep the box steady on her lap.

All the way home I kept telling Gail I should have asked Doug first, but I was afraid if I had waited until the next day, Sammy would be gone. Gail reassured me that Doug had grown up with cats and dogs, and he wasn't going to care if I brought a cat home.

I knew Gail was probably right: Doug would be fine with a cat. But me? Bringing a cat to our house? An indoor cat for someone with severe OCD? I must have lost my mind, but Enid's unexpected death had had a devastating effect on my sense of well being. I was not going to wait until I was an old lady dying in a nursing home before I held a cat again. I remember how I would be depressed or start crying every time I had seen a cat since I was a child.

Doug was shocked when we arrived home with Sammy. He was amazed that someone with a cleanliness fixation would bring home a pet. He was concerned about my being around an animal, and I'm sure he remembered some of my previous close encounters with animals. One especially traumatic one had happened a few years before in Leavenworth, a popular tourist town in the Cascade Mountains. We parked our car on the street while we had lunch in a restaurant. When we had finished eating, we saw a horse carriage in front of our car, waiting to give tourists rides. I wouldn't get near the horses, so I couldn't tell the owners to move them. And I didn't want Doug by the horses either. I stood there in the street, and since I didn't know anyone else and had no idea what to do, I started swearing and screaming. People walked by giving me a wide berth. I was surprised someone didn't call the police. I finally solved my problem by giving some teens ten dollars to take a carriage ride. I told them that if it didn't cost that much, they could keep the change. They agreed to take a ride after I explained to them I had OCD. They didn't know what it was, so I told them that I didn't want to get near the horses because they were dirty and they smelled. As soon as the carriage left the parking space and was turning the corner, Doug had to drive the car a block before I'd get in. All the way home, I was trying to convince myself that our car was not dirty as the horses had never touched it. Also I was lucky because they hadn't relieved themselves in the street. All horses in tourist areas should be required to have diapers as who wants to step in horse manure?

I could understand that Doug would be concerned for me. But Sammy is different than other animals. Sammy has helped me to become more calm even though I still avoid animals that are outside. And she helps me keep my perspective and live a normal life. In my mind, Sammy is clean because she is not exposed to dumpsters and other contaminated objects. Even her being on the floor doesn't make her dirty to me. Sammy can be on the rug and jump in my lap, and I don't feel as if my clothes are dirty. If Doug were to put a book on my lap that had been on the floor, I would want to change clothes immediately. It doesn't make any sense! There is a reason that OCD is called a *mental* illness.

So Gail had been right. Doug had no problems with a cat in our home once he saw I was okay with her. He loves her as much as I do, and she is now ten years old. We remember every August 29 that we got her in 1996. She is an old cat now and sleeps a lot, but she is still our pride and joy. I give her cat treats and scoop her up for naps. And Doug takes care of her litter box and feeding her.

Doug does a lot of the other jobs around the house. I can help with some household chores such as cooking, folding laundry, and doing the dishes. Doug saw how I would wash the counter top over and over again. I would also keep rinsing the dishes that I washed by hand over and over again with hot water until I was dripping wet with sweat. He tried to convince me to let him do the cleaning up after cooking, but I felt I should do it. After three years of marriage, Doug finally convinced me to let him do the cleanup. I would come from the kitchen swaying because I was so exhausted and overheated. Doug had taken over most of the other household chores and doing the few dishes by hand that did not go into the dishwasher was no problem for him.

I feel guilty because I don't do my share. I'm lucky to have an understanding husband who is patient with my rituals and listens to me. People with OCD need constant reassurance from loved ones that events in their lives are acceptable to live with. I ask Doug if I am contaminated from different objects and situations. His assures me I am not unclean. We both realize if he had lived in Wenatchee, I would never have dated him. I had the chance to know Doug because of a long-distance relationship.

"You know, Marie, I think I may have had the beginnings of OCD when I was young. If I had been in an environment where those tendencies were encouraged, I could have gotten OCD. I remember lining up all my shoes in the closet. And one day when I was washing my hands, I started washing the faucet handles over and over. My brother saw me and asked, 'What are you doing, Doug?' I mumbled something and stopped washing the faucet handles. I never did it again, but if I had seen someone in my family cleaning obsessively I could have become compulsive."

I was still having trouble with my stomach and burping a lot. Gail convinced me to see Dr. Dougan, their family doctor, who immediately sent me to a gastroenterologist. I had an ulcer and GERD. Dr. Chally told me that if I didn't do something about it, I would eventually be unable to swallow. I had to have four endoscopies over a period of a year and started taking medication for my ulcer. I was lucky I didn't require surgery.

The first year we lived in Minnesota I was ill. I lived in a haze under my drugs – Prozac, Lorazepam, and Premarin and Propulsid I was taking for my ulcer. After I started feeling better, I assisted at a career center at a junior-senior high school, but I had to quit because I would not use the public restroom. My life was severely handicapped by my mental illness. I was getting bored as I missed teaching. It is not easy to be a full-time teacher for 19 years and then do nothing. I was almost 44, and I became deeply depressed, and I was again not sleeping well.

I had a number of sleep complaints, including chronic tiredness and nightmares. One of my recurring nightmares found me in a building needing to use the toilet and not finding a clean bathroom. I would wake up panting and sweating. I also had chronic back pain and GERD.

Dr. Dougan referred me to the Sleep Center at Hennepin County Medical Center. Because of my past history of OCD, Dr. Davies at the center decided I needed to do an all-night sleep study. I stayed at the Sleep Center for one night in early February 1997. First, they'd look for sleep-disordered breathing. If sleep apnea wasn't the problem, I'd have a multiple sleep latency test (MLST) to look for the cause of my daytime sleepiness. If I had neither excessive tiredness nor daytime tiredness, then my dream life would be considered as a primary problem.

While being interviewed for my sleep problems, I told the doctor I thought I was getting enough sleep at night. Yet, I was tired the next day and took a nap. My chronic nightmares were related to my OCD. In them, I was always running away from some activity that distressed me. I would feel trapped and wake up feeling relieved that I was only having a nightmare but also exhausted from their paranoid

situations, including escaping contaminating situations and
being forced to do cleaning activities which would terrify
me, such as cleaning a bathroom or being in a basement
standing in a sewer backup. Dr. Davies thought that my
"perceived dream activities are actually intrusive thoughts
during wakefulness."

Doug told me I snored loudly and jerked during my
sleep. I know I jerk involuntarily when I am awake. I don't
think I have Tourette's Syndrome. However, swearing
uncontrollably as I did in Leavenworth when I saw the horse
carriage is also a part of Tourette's Syndrome. I can be
sitting reading a book, and all of a sudden I just jerk as if
I'm being zapped by electricity.

The all-night polysomnographic study and MLST concluded that I was suffering from a mild case of sleep apnea
which was treated with continuous positive airway pressure
(CPAP). My snoring increased to a crescendo followed by
apneic pauses. I had no evidence of hypersomnia, but I had,
according to Dr. Mahowald, "high voltage, slow eye movements [that] are seen during light non-REM sleep – most
likely representing current or prior SSRI (Selective Serotonin Reuptake Inhibitor) medication exposure." In other
words, the medication I was taking for OCD was a direct
factor in my ability to sleep. I already knew the medications
had side effects such as insomnia. Dr. Mahowald concluded
this "is an abnormal study" and suggested I use a nasal CPAP
machine to assist my sleeping, but I did not want to use any
breathing apparatus unless I had no choice. I still have problems sleeping, but I am able to continue functioning.

Doug's dad had become paralyzed from an aneurysm
in December 1998. We were constantly going to and from
the hospital. Ron was brought home in between medical
emergencies, and it was hard for Gail to take care of him.
Doug, his brother Dan, and I helped as much as possible,

but it was still a rough time for all of us. I felt so sorry for Ron as he was the one in the wheelchair. Many times I thought I would rather die than be in his place.

Doug was working almost full-time in the libraries. I didn't want him to work everyday as he did most of the house work at home and helped his Mom take care of his dad. Because of my compulsions and obsessions, I consider myself an invalid as far as being much help to Doug. His brother Dan had a job as an insurance adjuster, and he was overwhelmed with the amount of work required. I was glad I was able to go with Gail to the hospital because I didn't want her driving alone in Minneapolis, and I also enjoyed visiting Ron.

Doug was assigned to the inner city libraries. One day he was at work and saw an incident report on the desk stating shots had been fired at 2 a.m. and a body discovered in the library parking lot. The report stated that the body had been taken by the police to the funeral home across the street, and if it was not claimed, the city would pay for the burial. Another time Doug was working at the reference desk when he heard three gun shots. There was an elderly librarian sitting at the counter, and she just kept doing her work. Doug immediately dove over the top of the counter when he heard the shots. Doug exclaimed, "That sounded like gun shots!"

"It was," replied the little, old librarian with her hair wrapped in a bun on the top of her head.

"Are you just going to sit there?"

"Oh, it's okay; there's a crack house three doors up, and shots are often fired from the street or the house."

I was scared, and I didn't like Doug working in the libraries. Four of them were in areas where Doug refused to sub, but he was kept busy at the other libraries. I was depressed, bored, and tired of dealing with OCD. My life had again become a vicious cycle that I felt I had no control over. Doug was getting discouraged with what he had to deal with at work, so neither one of us was happy.

My extreme sadness became so great that I could no longer hide it in public. Doug's mom sold real estate, and we went with her to the company picnic in honor of all the employees and people who had bought houses. I was sitting at a table trying to eat a hot dog, and I couldn't quit crying. I was sobbing hysterically and telling Doug I didn't want to live. Gail decided I needed to go to the hospital. I was admitted to the psychiatric ward at Abbott-Northwestern hospital for depression, severe obsessive compulsive symptoms, and suicidal thoughts.

I was 46 and had gradually become completely exhausted from my compulsions. My state of mind led me to become withdrawn with frequent uncontrolled crying bouts and pessimistic thoughts about my life and the future. I was tired of the day to day routine of living. I wanted to crawl into a fetal position and forget the world even existed.

While I was in the hospital, I read my medical chart. I hadn't realized I could do that while still a patient. Those of us who wanted to read our own charts had to stay in the seating area in view of the front desk. I knew laws towards mental illness had changed over the years; a patient could request a copy of his medical chart after being discharged. What amazed me was being able to have access to this information before leaving the hospital. I read mine. I didn't object to anything written in my chart except I was angry that it stated I was "indifferently dressed and indifferently groomed."

I had gone straight from the picnic to the hospital, so I was not wearing my best clothes. In fact, I would never wear my best clothes to the hospital unless I had come directly from work. Having OCD, my casual clothes are usually easy to wash. I don't often buy clothes that need dry-cleaning, not only because I worry about how frequently these businesses change their cleaning fluid, but also because they put everything in long, plastic bags that are usually dragging on the floor as they return clothing. And I usually don't wear makeup because I don't think it is necessary. My hair, face, clothes, and body were clean. Excuse me? Is a female "indifferently groomed" because she isn't wearing makeup? I never commented to the staff about the "indifferently" wording.

I am very adept at adapting to any situation I am currently in, so after getting used to the hospital routine, I started talking to other patients. A man named Greg also had OCD, so we talked about cleanliness. If he was washing his hands and touched the sink, he would also have to start washing over again. Another patient named Mandy was admitted because she had threatened to kill her newborn baby. She really loved her baby, but found herself having thoughts of destroying her child. Her condition was diagnosed as postpartum depression.

In group therapy, we were encouraged to share experiences about our forms of mental illness. I told the group about an experience that had terrified me in 1980 while I was teaching class.

"I was sitting in my chair at my desk at school during second period. I was menstruating, and I could feel blood gushing on my sanitary napkin. I froze; I could not make myself stand up. I remained seated for the remaining 30 minutes of class. I must have looked sick, as two students asked me if I was okay. I stayed at my desk between classes even though teachers are supposed to be in the hallway. Ten minutes after third period started, the students were excused to attend a drama production. I waited until everyone was gone.

Next, I stood up and called the office using the phone intercom system. As I was standing, blood gushed down my leg dripping onto my shoe. The back of my dress was soaked with blood. I explained to Shirley, the secretary, what had happened.

"Shirley said, 'Don't worry, Marie. Drive home and if you're still gone when the students return from the play, someone will cover your class.'

"I panicked as I went through the halls. I had to walk the length of the school building before I could get to my car outside. I was so afraid a student would see me. Thank God, there wasn't anyone in the hall! I drove home as fast as I could. I changed clothes and arrived back at school just as the students were returning to the classrooms.

"My periods paralyzed me. I later decided to have a hysterectomy because my OCD caused me too much stress to cope with my periods. Besides, I never wanted to have children because of my cleanliness habits."

Jean, a bipolar patient, said, "Wow! You really went through an ordeal!"

"Yes, and it's an experience I didn't want to repeat."

Nick questioned, "Are you telling us you purposely had a hysterectomy, so you wouldn't have children?"

"I never wanted to put a child through the personal hell I live through everyday. I know the child would grow up hating me and with good reason."

"How do you feel about never having children?" asked Stacy.

"Most of the time I'm glad, but every time I see a child it reminds me of what I sacrificed. I try not to think about it; it's too painful."

The group of patients looked at me with pity in their eyes. I didn't want sympathy because it reinforced my hatred towards myself. My best coping mechanism is to avoid children, not only because it causes me sad memories, but also because in my mind babies and small children are contaminated.

This was my second time in a psychiatric ward. It had been so long, 16 years, since the first that I had forgotten how many symptoms could lead to dysfunction in people. It was a sobering thought for me because I realized again I was not the only one with problems. OCD patients, along with other mental patients, tend to focus narrowly on their own problems; it is important to be reminded that we are not alone and that others suffer their own personal hell. I knew focusing on my problem helped caused my depression. If I could become interested in something else, my anxiety would decrease. Boredom was an overwhelming problem for me because I still missed teaching. It made me angry I had to quit the career I loved; the anger caused my depression to increase creating a continuous cycle of self-loathing.

There are not many rooms open to all patients in a psychiatric ward. We were not allowed to visit someone in the bedrooms. Two patients shared a room, and the only other places we were able to congregate were in the TV lounge, eating area, and the arts and crafts room. Lisa, Kari, Meg, and I were drawing pictures of a vase with flowers. It was mundane work, but it is part of therapy to do different activities. The three of them had been admitted the day before, so I hadn't spent time with them until now.

"Why are you in here?" Kari asked Meg.

"I hadn't been able to sleep for three days and nights. The body ceases to function correctly from lack of sleep. The doctors are trying to adjust my medications, so I can return to a normal schedule of sleeping."

"What about you, Kari?" said Meg.

"I have severe panic attacks, especially when I'm in a car. Several times I have had to pull off the road and jump out of the car. I was hyperventilating while putting my head down on the trunk of the car. I knew I needed help, so here I am."

Lisa declared, "I'm here because I have anger management control problems. I become so angry I scream obscenities in public. I start shaking and lose control of my emotions."

I remarked, "I have OCD."

"What's that?" asked Meg.

"It's obsessive compulsive disorder. I'm obsessed with cleanliness and avoiding anything that I think will make me feel unclean. Some people with OCD are constantly checking to see if the stove is off, or they are counting over and over again the number of steps they have taken to get to a room. My obsession is very debilitating as it constantly disrupts my life."

"Well," said Kari, "it sounds like all of us are at the right place. I just hope I don't have to stay here too long because the confinement is driving me crazy!"

I was given Level II privileges, which gave me more freedom to move about the hospital because I could leave the locked ward. I was so happy to be able to take the elevator from the "prison" to the first floor. I had escaped if only for 30 minutes! I decided to treat myself to French fries at the McDonalds near the registration desk in the front lobby. Sitting in a booth close to the counter, I observed people. Everyone was involved in their daily lives; I felt excluded and irredeemable. Humans don't know what it's like to be in a "gilded cage" unless they have personally experienced it for themselves.

It was exhilarating to be free, and I walked the first floor of the hospital until my half hour of freedom expired. I wanted to be released from my "cage." I realized the psychiatric department was always on the top floor if the hospital was a tall building. Thinking to myself that the location where mental patients were incarcerated was no accident, I dejectedly forced myself to return to the psychiatric wing. Depression overwhelmed me as I pushed the button to reenter the elevator from the first floor. After the elevator stopped and I exited, I had to push another button to alert the staff I wanted to reenter. I panicked at the thought of checking back into confinement; I wanted to return to the elevator and leave the hospital. A nurse pushed the inside button, and the locked door opened to allow me to walk back into the ward. I automatically reentered and was trapped again.

I was eventually assigned to Level III, which restricted my privileges to the Crises Management Program because I was having trouble adjusting to Seroquel. I was experiencing continual "quasi-delusional symptoms" associated with germs and concerns about hygiene and diagnosed with a "hypo manic mood." I walked around the ward with zombie-like movements, as it was an effort for me to put one foot in front of the other. I fell and was rocking back and forth in the fetal position. I was immobilized, and my bizarre behavior alarmed me. Dr. Vydas determined that I might have "cyclic mood swings," so he prescribed Depakote. I started improving, and my dosage was increased. I continued to ameliorate on the mood stabilizer and was discharged on June 23, 1999.

I was given instructions to do follow-up consultations with a psychiatrist. I wanted one near my residence rather than continue with one at the hospital. I didn't want to drive into downtown Minneapolis because I dislike being in a city environment. I panic when I am on a city street because there is nowhere to go if I see something that upsets me. I usually can adapt to suburbs because they are cleaner and have wider streets in case I feel the need to escape a situation.

I was lackadaisical with my follow-up sessions with a psychiatrist. I went only because I needed a doctor to write prescriptions for my medications. Exhausted from coping with my mental illness, I wanted to sleep, not talk.

CHAPTER SEVENTEEN

Doug was tired of dealing with Minnesota weather, mosquitoes, state taxes, and the inner city libraries. We decided to move back to Washington State to Mill Creek, north of Seattle. During the first three years of our marriage when Doug had moved to Washington, he had enjoyed our mild climate. Even eastern Washington winters are preferable to Minnesota winters, especially in January and February. On the west side of the Cascades it doesn't snow often, but there is plenty of rain. However, as Doug says, "You don't have to shovel the rain."

We arrived in Mill Creek in August 1999. Doug and I had flown to Seattle to find a house the previous month. His mom came with us and helped us find a nice place. We settled in with our cat Samantha, and Doug started subbing at the local high school. I was happy because we had moved back to Washington, and I was dealing well with my OCD. We immediately started seeing a general practitioner named Dr. Billet as we both needed to continue our medications. Doug took only two pills to help him sleep, but I needed to stay stable. Dr. Billet recommended a psychiatrist to me. I started seeing him, but he was very distant. I sat in a chair just inside his office door, and he stayed at his desk in the far corner. He kept calling me Maria, instead of Marie. I felt isolated and ignored. He wasn't any help to me, so I quit seeing him.

When Doug does a thorough housecleaning, I go to the library as it bothers me to be present when he cleans the bathrooms and floors and vacuums the rug. I also don't watch him when he is doing the dishes after I have cooked because if I did, I would see him doing something that I would consider dirty. I don't want him to have to repeat the cleaning he has just finished, so I find it easier not to observe him and assume everything is done correctly. I once heard about a woman who would make her son wear old clothes to take out the garbage; he had to take them off outside before he came in the house to take a shower. Another woman made her daughter study in a closet after school because she thought her daughter's school books were contaminated. I was glad medication had calmed me enough where I didn't make Doug change clothes every time he took out the garbage. Doug always takes a shower and puts on clean clothes if he has been cleaning for several hours. He said he would take a shower even if I didn't request him to take one because he perspires heavily while doing housework. I'm glad he takes a shower not to humor me but because he feels the need to be clean.

By late February of 2000, I was feeling depressed again. I had stopped taking Dapakote which had been prescribed for me the previous June when I was at Abbott Northwestern Hospital in Minneapolis. I was still taking Zoloft and Amitriptyline. My medications were still being prescribed by Dr. Billet. I know patients are not supposed to discontinue medications without medical advice, but I, like thousands of other patients, would decide that some pill wasn't helping me and quit taking it. I probably didn't give

Dapakote enough time to work. I also needed to see another psychiatrist, but every place I called had doctors who weren't taking new patients.

One of the reasons for my depression was the side effects caused by taking medications. I felt nothing when Doug and I were intimate. Between having a hysterectomy and the pills I had been taking for several years, I was unable to enjoy sex. I was frustrated, and doctors would give me different pills to help overcome sexual dysfunction. Nothing worked for me, and I was not willing to take an extra medication on a long term basis because I was already taking 12 pills a day.

One day I saw an announcement on television advertising a research study for depression and psychosis starting in March. Dr. Khan, at the Northwest Clinical Research Center in Bellevue, was looking for people willing to take part in a double blind study where they would be taking either Olanzapine, Fluoxetine, or a placebo for the management of depressive symptomatology. I called the number listed and went for my first appointment on March 21.

Dr. Shioto asked me to complete a lengthy questionnaire. Next she interviewed me and asked if I could return two days later for a blood test. She explained the blood test was necessary to determine if a person was free of illegal drugs. Part of the study would also require me to be in the psychiatric ward of Overlake Hospital from March 30 through April 6. I wasn't thrilled about going to another psychiatric ward, but I thought it might help me with my depression because I was feeling hopeless and suicidal.

I had the blood test and was accepted into the study. On March 30 I was admitted to Overlake Hospital and escorted to the psychiatric ward. I had become familiar with the routine required to be a patient. While I was being interviewed, I avoided touching any items in the interview room, including door knobs. I would not shake hands with the nurse. My hands were red and dry from frequent washings. All my belongings were checked to make sure I hadn't brought something harmful to myself or others, and I was assigned a room. The aide showed me where towels, bathrobes, pajamas, and other supplies were located. I was in a double room with a bathroom connecting to another double room. I was upset that I had to share a bathroom with three other people instead of just one person. Fortunately the rooms had sinks, so I wouldn't be observed by more than one person when I washed my hands. The connecting bathroom had a toilet and shower stall.

My medical chart stated, "the patient was quite anxious and fearful upon admission, but made a very earnest attempt in participating in all group and milieu therapy. The patient missed at most one group per day, due to being tied up in her one hour long shower." My chart also stated that I was "casually dressed with no grooming." Again, I thought it was ridiculous to say I had no grooming just because I wasn't wearing makeup. Psychiatrists and psychologists need to reword their observations when referring to females. I cannot imagine them stating that a male had no grooming because he wasn't wearing makeup. My appearance was immaculate but not made up with artificial products.

The food at Overlake Hospital was good. I had been encouraged to increase my fluid and food intake, so I ate heartily. I went from 148 pounds to 156 pounds by the time I was discharged. I thought I might as well eat because I was taking daily showers anyway. Part of my problem can be attributed to not eating enough food to sustain me. Naturally I am happier and feeling better when I eat correctly.

I called Doug every day, but I did not want him to visit me as he would then become contaminated. He was lonely, but he understood my need to get more help. I was bored

attending group meetings where patients discussed everything from mood swings to methods of self-relaxation, but I
felt I needed to participate in the groups because my hospi-
talization was being paid by the clinical research center.

I socialized with everyone during meal times, and I
was beginning to enjoy myself as I am an extrovert. One
woman interested me because she had bipolar disorder,
which used to be called manic depressive. I was conversing
with Karen about her disorder when she suddenly stopped
talking and stared off into the distance. I realized that part
of her illness was losing her train of thought and not being
aware she had stopped talking.

Another woman named Becky suffered from severe
narcolepsy; she would be talking to someone and fall into a
deep sleep. Karen, the bipolar patient, angrily snapped during group therapy that if Becky fell asleep one more time,
she was sure she was going to smack her. One of the other
patients explained Becky's condition. I know patients are
not suppose to ask the staff about other patients, but in
this case I thought the staff should have explained to us
about her sleepiness as I was dismayed Karen wanted to
hit Becky. Yet, Becky's condition was not meant to be public knowledge. Most patients will discuss with other
patients why they are in the hospital, but some want to
keep their privacy.

Adult patients had to share the dining and recreation
areas with teenage patients. It bothered me because whenever I am around kids, I automatically feel as if I have to
be a chaperon. This is ingrained in me from 19 years of
teaching. A teenager named Barb, who had trichotilloma-
nia (pulling one's hair out over and over), was especially
obnoxious. She and a group of her friends would try to
annoy the adult patients. It is hard enough coping with
mental illness; putting young people with adults adds more

stress as they are still kids and are going to act accordingly. One teenage boy was cussing and had to be put in the locked room for unruly patients. I could hear his screams as I walked around the ward.

My mental health improved daily, and I no longer was feeling hopeless or suicidal. I was discharged on April 6 and continued to participate in the research study conducted by Dr. Kahn. My next appointment was April 11. It is frustrating participating in a blind study because one doesn't know if one is taking real pills or placebos. I didn't like having blood tests taken every time.

Meanwhile, Doug's dad Ron had surgery again on April 14. We were both stressed as we didn't know whether Doug was going to be needed again in Minnesota. I continued the research study during the month of April.

Doug flew to Minneapolis on May 2. He was supposed to return May 11, but he had to stay longer. I relapsed when Doug left. I continued the study, but I was agoraphobic, felt unsafe, panicked, and was suicidal. I quit the research study and was admitted to Fairfax Hospital on May 19. Another psychiatric ward! This was the fourth one I had been admitted to, the third one within the last year. I was appalled because the shower faucet in the bathroom was an erratic stream of water that didn't get me as clean as I wanted to be. I was put in a room with three other patients, but I immediately requested a room with only one roommate. After two days, I was able to change rooms because one of the patients was transferred to another hospital

Fairfax had two separate wards, one for adults and one for adolescents, but we ate in a communal dining hall. I liked the staff and appreciated the fact the hospital was attached to a school the teenagers attended. It had a gym where we were allowed to play volleyball. I feel better if I am participating in sports. I didn't care if the ball touched the gym floor because I felt contaminated anyway in the hospital setting.

Doug was still in Minnesota, and I was still depressed. If I'd been home, I'd have been stressed because of his absence. But being in the psychiatric ward was worse because I felt so contaminated by it.

CHAPTER EIGHTEEN

I was discharged from Fairfax on May 24, 2000. I drove home to our house in Mill Creek. My car was contaminated from my having been in the germ-ridden hospital, so I had to clean the interior. I put all the clothes I had taken with me to the hospital in the laundry and took a long shower. The next morning I decided to go to my Mom's duplex in Quincy because I was unstable. I did not trust myself to be alone while Doug was gone. For years I had not driven a long distance by myself without someone else helping me to drive. I was shaky by the time I got to Issaquah. I pulled into a fast food place and forced myself to eat a hamburger, French fries, and a strawberry milkshake. I was crying hysterically, and I had difficulty breathing and eating. I continued driving even though I was hyperventilating and crying. I had to pull over and rest several times before I arrived in Quincy.

I was erratic, and because I wasn't thinking clearly, I had not brought enough medications with me. I thought I would be all right as long as I spent time with Mom and ate well. I decided I would stay with Mom until Doug returned from Minnesota. I begged him to come home early, but he had to help take care of his dad. Doug thought I would be safe now that I was with Mom.

There is a reason family members are not supposed to treat other family members. Being so emotionally close to the patient makes one lose perspective of the care the patient needs. I didn't realize I need consistently to take the proper dosage of my medications to remain stable, and neither did my mom. Since I hadn't brought enough pills for my stay, I ran out. My mom didn't understand the extent of my mental illness and how important my medication is. If she had, she would have ordered more pills for me. I don't blame her because I thought I was doing better, but I wasn't thinking properly. I knew I was becoming more unstable every day, but I thought I would be able to cope for a few days without my pills. My reasoning was faulty as I should never be without medications.

Finally May 30 arrived, and I told Mom I was driving back and staying by the airport so I could pick up Doug the next day. But I was shaky and weak. I told Mom that I didn't think I'd be able to drive. I was afraid I'd get in an accident before I'd driven ten miles.

Mom took one look at me and announced, "I'll drive you back."

"But, Mom, you don't see well anymore, and you'd have to fly home."

But Mom was determined. She could see I was in no condition to drive myself home. I was so proud of Mom as she drove all the way without stopping once. We stayed at the Doubletree Inn by SeaTac Airport. We were on the 14th floor of the hotel, and I wanted to open the door to the balcony and jump off. The only reason I didn't jump was because Doug was coming home. The next morning Mom and I met Doug at the arrival gate. I was having trouble walking because I was shaking, weak, and off my medications. I could barely follow Doug and Mom to the baggage retrieval area. Doug was alarmed at my appearance. Again, I don't think Mom realized how ill I was, as even I didn't realize I was in a stupor. I was muttering to myself and finding it hard to continue standing. Mom flew back to eastern Washington and Doug drove me to Mill Creek.

I resumed taking my medications once I was home, and Doug made me promise never to run out of them again. "Even if you have to call your doctor and have him call the local pharmacy, I don't want you to be without your pills."

I knew he was right; I'd been crazy to think I could maintain my health without my pills. I tried to remain calm, but I had been in a state of hysteria for too long. Seven days later on June 7, 2000, I put a gun in my mouth and pulled the trigger.

CHAPTER NINETEEN

Mom never admitted to having OCD. The closest she came to ever saying anything remotely related is when she once told my husband, "I may have overdone the cleaning when I was raising the kids."

Mom also felt she had no part in my OCD or the effects it had on me. She once told me, "I hope you know none of this has anything to do with me."

The "this" she was referring to was my attempted suicide. On June 7, 2000, when I could no longer cope with being alive, I put a gun in my mouth and pulled the trigger. Nothing happened. I took the gun out of my mouth and cocked the gun again. Nothing happened for the second time. I then put the gun back in the drawer. When my husband came home ten minutes later, I told him what I had done. He insisted that I go to the hospital, and for the fifth time in my life, I was put in a psychiatric ward. This time was different as the four previous times were voluntary admissions. I was taken to the emergency room and put on a gurney while I waited for an initial assessment before being admitted to the involuntary section of the psychiatric ward. There was a policeman with a patient that had come from jail. The policeman asked me if there was anything he could do to help.

"Yeah, give me your gun, so I can kill myself."

He wasn't surprised, but he didn't offer to help me either. Thoughts of suicide remained on my mind. I wanted to find a high place to jump off of – a bridge or the top of the hospital. I was very negative and did not want to stay.

After lying in a bed in an admitting room for an hour, a medical social representative arrived. Angry and confused as to why I was being forced to stay, I was not cooperative. I had seen my psychiatrist, Dr. Salmon, the previous week. I had been unstable when I had seen him, but I have learned over the years how to be a great actress. I had agreed to start seeing him on a regular basis. And I had assured him that I was doing well.

I was not. Depression over Doug's absence coupled with my lack of medication pushed me to the edge. Coming on the heels of my previous hospitalizations – Abbott Northwestern in Minneapolis in June 1999, Overlake Hospital in Bellevue in April 2000, and Fairfax Hospital in May 2000 – were obvious signs that I was only getting worse. Then came June 7 when I put the gun in my mouth. I was disgusted to be forced into the psychiatric ward when I had not agreed to be there. Depressed, I was not ready to be cooperative. This was the third time in less than four months that I was hospitalized in a psychiatric ward, and this time I had not done so voluntarily. I did not want to check in. This had been Doug's idea, and the staff had agreed with him. So even though I wanted to leave, I was emotionally vulnerable and felt overwhelmed by the events. I just gave in to the pressure to be admitted. But I was incensed. How dare the medical system – or anyone – force me to stay where I did not want to remain!

I was taken to the ward on the top floor of the hospital, and since Dr. Salmon had seen me the week before, he became my psychiatrist. I was impressed he never said anything about my having reassured him the previous week that I was going to be all right.

Dr. Salmon asked me, "What day is today?"

"Today is June 7, 2000."

"How old are you?"

"Forty-seven."

"How many fingers am I holding up?"

"What did you say?"

"Marie, I want you to tell me how many fingers I am holding up."

"Three fingers."

"Do you see objects that aren't there?"

"Like hallucinations? No, I don't see things."

"Do you hear voices?"

"No, I just have OCD."

Dr. Salmon performed a general examination with a nurse present that included checking my eyes, chest, heart, and abdomen. The charts I requested from the hospital after I was released stated that I was "alert, awake and oriented. [I was] diagnosed as suicidal ideation attempt and depression."

Being in the involuntary ward made me hostile. Three of the five hospitals I had been in did not have separate wards for voluntary versus involuntary patients. Everyone was just thrown together, and some of the patients scared me. It would seem logical that I would be safer in the voluntary side of the psychiatric ward because I was not psychotic. Instead, I was forced to be in the ward with involuntary patients because I was considered a danger to myself and other patients. Eventually I could go over to the voluntary side if I met certain criteria. I was informed

I might have to have a court hearing before I could leave. At least the hearing would take place at the hospital with a lawyer representing me. But I never had a hearing, as I was released by Dr. Salmon a week later.

My condition was observed to be "in no gross physical distress....neatly but casually dressed and groomed, wearing no makeup....hair was cut in the style of a pageboy haircut. Psychomotor activity was somewhat restless. Mood appeared to be anxious and depressed. Thought content revealed no delusions and no illusions."

My chart stated, "The patient was initially thought to be suffering from major depression, recurrent, non psychotic." I informed the staff that I was not sleeping well, and I was bored. I had looked around the hospital, and I couldn't find a way to commit suicide so I told them I "was not suicidal."

I felt trapped and resented it. All I could think about was escaping. I wanted out right now, but I knew I had to be there at least 48 hours for observation. Since I had been admitted without my consent, my stay would be even longer. I wore hospital clothing as I was too depressed to get dressed every day. I would not look at my caregivers if I could help it. The food was unappealing; I threw up one night while trying to eat dinner. All the patients sat watching TV, looking depressed. A woman named Cindy kept swearing. Dr. Salmon told her she would have to behave if she wanted to progress in her treatment. She evidently didn't want to advance because she continued to swear and yell at the staff. I was impressed when Dr. Salmon ignored her.

Sitting in the lounge one afternoon, I started talking to a patient named Steve.

He declared, "I have MPD."

"What does that stand for?"

"It means multiple personality disorder; I have three completely and distinct persons within my body. I am Joe, who is meek. I am myself, who is apathetic. I am Ryan, who is aggressive and full of hate."

I didn't know how to respond. I sat in silence for several moments and then remarked, "How do you cope with all of your personalities?"

"I don't do well; that's why I'm here."

"Do you know what OCD is?"

"Yeah, is that what you have?"

"Yes, so I'm trying to understand what it must be like to have MPD."

"Well," Steve replied, "it isn't easy, but I know OCD isn't easy either because my sister has it."

I felt sorry for Steve, but I was in no condition to deal with his mental problems. I couldn't even cope with my own. I went back to my room, crawled under the covers, and avoided the world. Of course, my solution to my problem didn't work as nurses kept disturbing me with medications to take and telling me I shouldn't sleep all the time.

After two days, I felt ready to attend meetings on the open unit. These meetings are all the same with everyone sitting around trying to get in touch with their feelings and what brought them to the hospital. This was the third time in a three-month period I had been in a psychiatric ward, and I was sick of being in meetings.

I also had to attend a conference with my doctor and my close relatives. Doug told my mom and Leslie to come over for the family conference. He was upset because he had to convince them to come over as they didn't realize the severity of my situation. Leslie and Mom were used to my psychiatric hospitalizations, but the difference this time was that I had attempted suicide. Doug called a family friend to convince them to come over to Edmonds. It took them four hours to drive to the hospital.

Leslie was shocked when she entered the ward and saw me sitting in the activities room doing watercolors. "How can you do that? This is not my sister sitting here."

The conference was held in a private room with Dr. Salmon, Doug, my mom, and Leslie. My dad had died nine years before, and my brother was too far away to attend. My family was concerned about my safety and how my OCD was affecting me. They also reminded me it was a sin to commit suicide, so I guess they were also concerned about my spiritual safety.

I was curled up in a ball on a couch by myself as I felt contaminated being in the hospital. I wouldn't let my husband give me a kiss or let my family hug me. I didn't want them to become contaminated. Hospitals are full of germs, and I couldn't wait to get out of this contaminating environment. Dr. Salmon noted on my chart that "much concern was expressed about [the patient's] safety and her obsessive compulsive disorder. Her father was described as a man who fended off his child rearing responsibility to their mother. The patient expressed a wish to be discharged from the hospital soon."

I was on a constant merry-go-round without the choice of ever slowing down or escaping. Was there any way to get out of this chaos called OCD? The only way to get rid of all the agony, hate, pity, and sorrow was by ending my life. I had reached that point when I had put the gun in my mouth. I knew it was a cowardly way to deal with my problem, but I didn't care anymore. I just wanted to stop feeling anything, and I didn't want to live another minute where I would be concerned about keeping clean. I tried to force my thoughts back to the present which meant focusing on getting well.

Most of the conference revolved around my sister, Mom, and my husband asking me how I could attempt suicide. I felt really bad, as I hadn't left a note for Doug explaining why I wanted to end it all. I was so depressed that I never took the time to say goodbye. I knew this was not a good way to end my life because the police look first at the remaining spouse as a possible suspect for death. I was sure with all my history of psychiatric hospitals and sessions with doctors over the years that nothing would happen to Doug. Still, I should have left a note to clarify everything. The letter would have said the following:

> *Dear Doug,*
>
> *I can't stand living anymore. I'm sick and tired of dealing with OCD.*
>
> *When I resigned from teaching, I had no idea how my not working would bother me. For 19 years I had been teaching over 140 students a day and then NOTH-ING. The first year after I resigned, I didn't care I wasn't working since I was too busy recovering my health. When we moved to Minnesota, I spent the first year trying to get well. Then I helped in a career center. But that was no substitute for my teaching full-time. As time went on, I felt more and more worthless. There's a lot to be said for having someplace to work and contributing to society.*
>
> *I feel useless. My life has no meaning. I don't want to live anymore. I love you very much, but I hate my life and going on and on and on does not appeal to me. I want to die and end it all.*
>
> *I don't want you to feel responsible. You have been a good husband, and it is not your fault.*
>
> *Love,*
> *Marie*

I didn't write a note. I just put the gun in my mouth. After I put the gun back where it belonged, I got in bed and huddled in the fetal position until Doug came home. He forced me to go to the hospital. I later found out that I had not chambered a round. I had not practiced with the gun for three years, and I still don't know what I did wrong not to make the gun fire. I DON'T WANT TO KNOW WHAT I DID WRONG BECAUSE I AM HOPING THAT I NEVER WANT TO KILL MYSELF AGAIN.

Most women, according to statistics, will try and commit suicide by overdosing on pills because they want to look good in the coffin. I didn't care about looking nice; I just wanted to blow my head off. Besides, I was afraid if I took pills I would overdose, and the medics would save me. I would be a "vegetable" the rest of my life with permanent brain damage. I wanted a quick and irreversible solution.

My mind had been wandering, and I forced myself to return my attention to the conference Dr. Salmon was leading with my family.

"How could you do this to us?" my mom asked. "You know it's a sin to commit suicide."

I sat huddled on a corner of the couch hardly looking at my family. I wanted to scream that I didn't care about anything anymore. I wanted to tell Mom again, as I had many times before, that she was the reason I wanted to die. My adrenaline was in overdrive.

Leslie kept saying, "This isn't my twin sitting here who was in the arts and crafts room doing watercolors. Marie, what is wrong with you? You need to live for Doug and for your cat, Samantha. She needs her mom."

Dr. Salmon kept writing notes and saying that the others weren't helping me by making me feel guilty. But they didn't seem to hear his words.

Doug continued laying on the guilt. "How could you not say goodbye? Why did you want to end it all? I love you and want you to stay alive."

I know my family was just concerned about me and wanted to be sure I would be safe. That's why Doug was angry when I was released from the hospital by Dr. Salmon on June 15 after only eight days. I had shown clinical progress and felt safe to return home. My hospital duration was determined by Dr. Salmon, not by Doug. I self-rated my mood at seven on a scale from zero to ten with ten being the highest.

I told Dr. Salmon that I really loved my husband. He had called me about my suicidal expressions, and told me he had been crying while talking to the telephone answering service about fearing that I would eventually commit suicide. I felt terrible about the stress Doug had to endure, but I wasn't able to do anything about it. I was to continue seeing Dr. Salmon for outpatient therapy.

Doug discussed a longer hospital stay with Dr. Salmon. "More than just a week or two, perhaps up to six weeks. She might need electroconvulsive therapy."

I had no intention of receiving shock treatments.

On the final day I was in the hospital, I asked Dr. Salmon if my prescriptions could be called to the pharmacy. I felt contaminated, and if I handed the written prescriptions to the pharmacist, then I would think I was contaminating the pharmacist's hands along with the medications he would prepare. Doctors hear and see all kinds of behaviors; I am sure Dr. Salmon thought this was a strange request, but he complied. I was smiling by the time I was dismissed, and "was not thought to represent an imminent risk of harm to [my]self or others."

Doug thought I wasn't doing well when I returned home. He was still angry that I had been released so soon. We had always slept in separate rooms because of my snoring, but I had no idea how much my condition was still bothering him until he wrote a letter dated June 29, 2000, to one of Mom's friends. The letter was returned to our address because it had a wrong address. The letter said the following:

> Dear Mary,
>
> It is hard for me to believe that on June 7th Marie went through my closet, found one of my automatic pistols, then went through a chest of drawers for bullets. Marie then loaded a bullet into the clip, then locked the clip in, then put it in her mouth, and pulled the trigger — twice! As the round wasn't loaded into the breech, nothing happened. Not knowing what to do, I took her to Stevens Hospital. There she was admitted under court order for 30 days.
>
> The next week, Dr. Salmon, Marie's psychiatrist, wanted a family conference. Leslie didn't want to come; neither did Margaret. I had to contact Margaret's sister, Dorothy, and Butch (her accountant she trusts), to get them to attend the family conference. They did not stay 48 hours. They have been of absolutely no help during this crisis.
>
> When they did come, Margaret and Leslie also decided to 'spring' Marie. The court-ordered 30 days, in fact, became eight. I'll tell you, money talks and bull shit walks! In some ways, I wish they hadn't interfered with court orders. I wish Marie could have gotten the help she needs and adjusted to her new medications!
>
> Marie is now on massive dosages (the highest allowed) of Lorazepam, Prozac, and Anaphranil. I have been told she is still a danger to herself, but also that she is a danger to others. Thus, I have been sleeping with a bar stool propped in front of the door. Many times, I have been startled in the middle of the night thinking Marie is

trying to come in. If you remember the movie Psycho with
Norman Bates, you have an idea of what my fears are.

I am VERY sorry to dump such a letter as this on
you. But my family and friends are in Minnesota. I've
had to deal with this situation by myself. Albert and Darla
have, however, called or e-mailed every day. Marie said
that if there should ever arise a difficulty or issue, I should
contact you. Somehow, just getting this off my chest has
made me feel better. I really shouldn't have to deal with
this situation alone. Any advice, understanding you can
give me from your years of knowing this family will be
appreciated. I remind myself of the vow I took before
God, which says, "for better or worse." Well, I don't rightly
see how much worse it can get. Say a prayer.

Sincerely,
Doug Spaulding

I didn't know Doug had written the letter until it was
returned. I was glad it hadn't been delivered because I know
it would have embarrassed Mom and Leslie. I can't blame
Doug for expressing his true feelings as it had to be frustrating to cope with my condition. I know I have put Doug
through hell with my OCD; he has been a good husband
and has gone the distance with me.

Doug's letter was not entirely accurate as money had
nothing to do with my being discharged eight days after I
was admitted to the hospital. I would have been transferred
to the voluntary side of the psychiatric ward if there had
been any beds available before I left. I wasn't required to
have a court hearing as my condition improved. Mom and
Leslie had nothing to do with my getting out early; the
30-day time period for confinement had been dismissed.

I continued to see Dr. Salmon, and Doug relaxed more. We went on with our lives knowing that we had survived a maelstrom.

I received a note from a friend named Bob.

> *Marie, you are one of the kindest and most genuine persons I have met. You have had a positive impact on so many people, literally hundreds, by what you say and how you live. I have always felt that the Lord has a plan for all of us. Sometimes it is difficult for me to understand what that plan is, or how I fit into it. Yet, I know that our time in this world is limited, and that a better world awaits us. This world will be a lonelier place without you. More important, there are undoubtedly people out there who you have yet to meet and who likewise will be blessed with your friendship and company. Please know Doug and you are in our prayers. We wish you the best in your recovery and offer any support that might be helpful to you.*

Sometimes a crisis is the only way to get a message through. My attempted suicide let those close to me as well as my medical advisors know how serious I felt my situation really was. But it also gave others the opportunity to let me know how much I was loved and needed. I realize I had tremendous support from family and friends.

CHAPTER TWENTY

I have been seeing Dr. Salmon since I was discharged from Stevens Hospital. He has been a tremendous help to me, especially with my resentment because I am no longer teaching. He keeps reminding me, "You are not retired; you are disabled." This helps me to control my guilt because I am not working. He also reminds me that "having children is not the answer to problems."

I keep reminding myself how I never wanted to put a child through the hell I had experienced since I was 11. I am happy most of the time with the fact that I do not have any children, but sometimes the decision I made depresses me. I also feel guilty when I have bad thoughts, but Dr. Salmon reminds me, "You can't control how you feel; you *can* control what you do."

The happiest time of my life was when I was ten. I didn't know I had any problems concerning cleanliness, and I felt warm, protected, loved, and safe because I had two parents who cared about me. At ten I wasn't worried about dating or my appearance. I was just having fun being a kid.

One day in therapy, Dr. Salmon asked me, "Do you blame your father for any of your problems with OCD?"

The question astonished me but I replied, "No. Dad did not reinforce our habits." However, Doug thought of an interesting point that I hadn't considered. Mom and Dad came from the generation where the mother stayed home with the children and the father worked. When we entered elementary school, Mom wanted to work two days a week at the hospital to keep up professionally with the latest nursing methods. Dad wouldn't let her because he didn't want his wife working outside the home.

Doug said, "Maybe your dad should have let your mom work; it would have given her an outlet. She may not have cleaned so much if she had had the hospital environment to help occupy her mind."

Doug is perceptive; I think he found a reason for Mom's obsession, as she had nothing to do but focus her attention on her house, husband, and children. She did help with blood drawings and vaccinations, but it was piecemeal work and wasn't fulfilling. I loved my Mom, and I know she did not have a happy marriage. Dad provided well for his family, but all Mom ever wanted was to be treated as the queen of her castle as her married friends were. Dad also was not happy; the friction between my parents became obvious to me as I grew older.

A friend of Leslie's pointed out to her, "Since your dad died in 1991, it seems that you three siblings are finally living your own lives. Al and Marie both got married in 1993, and, now, Leslie, you're getting married in 1996."

When Leslie told me what Maggie had said, it really made me think. I knew Dad had a very controlling influence in our lives, but it was an epiphany for me to realize others understood to some extent what the three of us had dealt with as children and adults.

Doug would continuously tease me about my weight; I now weighed 156 pounds. I know Doug is concerned about my health, but I don't want to hear how much I weigh all the time. I'm well aware of it without his comments. Leslie weighs 20 pounds less than I do, and I feel awkward when I am standing next to her as people are always comparing identical twins.

I am no longer afraid to tell strangers about my OCD. I find most people try to be understanding even if they don't really know the debilitating effects of mental illness. When I buy clothing, I will fold it before I give it to the clerk. I explain I have OCD; I do not want the clerk to fold the clothing because most people are careless. They drag the clothing against their body, or they let the clothing touch the floor while they are folding it.

If a waitress drops something, I will sometimes ask for another waitress. I will leave a restaurant if I haven't ordered yet and someone working there is vacuuming or dusting. It's grotesque to be cleaning one minute and serving food the next minute. Restaurant workers shouldn't be doing any extra cleaning when they have customers. Vacuuming, even using the silent sweepers, is unnecessary. I have yet to see an employee wash after cleaning. The person continues setting tables and serving food even though it is not hygienic. Health inspectors should be stricter to prevent more illnesses.

For a while I joined the local women's club and a book club. I was very nervous at luncheons because women bring purses and put them on the floor next to them. Then they put the purses in their laps and put them on the floor again. I did not want any purses touching me. I also didn't want book club members handing me materials about the books being discussed because most people keep everything on the floor. I attended only four luncheons before I became too upset to continue going to them. I quit the book club after one year even though I had been enjoying the book discussions. My continual fear of becoming contaminated forced me to quit activities that I enjoyed.

It is now April 2005, and I have finished this book. I am still coping with OCD to the best of my ability. I know I will have this mental illness until I die. My main goal is to stay out of psychiatric wards because I am tired of not being in control. I continue to see Dr. Salmon; he helps me maintain my sanity. I have made a promise to myself that I will never stop taking my pills again or let my prescriptions expire. I have learned by painful experience how important therapy and medications are for my mental health.

I continue to have panic attacks and nightmares. Sometimes I awaken, shaking and dripping with sweat. I will scream and swear if I am in a situation I find intolerable. I try to deal with each day separately, as thinking about the future stresses me to the point of exhaustion. Each day is a repeat of the day before. I constantly worry if I am being contaminated; I approach every situation with caution. I try to foresee possible scenarios, and then I do my best to avoid anything happening that would upset me.

In many ways, OCD is a crippling condition. I could not handle it without my doctors, friends, priest, family, Sammy, and especially, Doug. I am constantly aware of the love that surrounds me and allows me to get through each day.

For further information about OCD:
OCF (Obsessive Compulsive Foundation)
676 State Street
New Haven, CT 06511
phone: 203 401-2070 fax: 203 401-2076